Making Friends of Enemies

Reflections on the teachings of Jesus

Jim Forest

Crossroad • New York

To Nancy

'We already stand on the hidden ground of love'
— Thomas Merton

1988

The Crossroad Publishing Company
370 Lexington Avenue, New York, N.Y. 10017

Printed in the United States of America

Library of Congress Cataloging-in-Publication Data

Forest, James H.
  Making friends of enemies.

  Bibliography: p.
  1. Love—Religious aspects—Christianity. 2. Jesus
Christ—Teachings. I Title.
BV4639.F58   1987   241'.4   87-36482
ISBN 0-8245-0885-8

Contents

Preface

'Once upon a time, in a very big city, there was a man who lived alone in his apartment. When he got home from his day of work, thinking of all the violent and dangerous people he had been close to that day on the streets, on buses and subways, he felt like a survivor of war. The most frightening minutes of all were those spent alone in the hallway unlocking the four locks on his door. This took only one or two minutes, though it always seemed much longer. The main lock was especially costly and had quite a special key. He often suspected this was where some killer would shoot him — as he fumbled with his keys at the door trying to open the last lock. Once inside, he re-fastened the four locks, then pushed home the two bolts, and finally attached the chain. Safe inside, he made his supper and then watched television. Whether he watched news or movies, it was always the same — war, murder, rape and robbery. He kept the lights low and the heavy curtains drawn. It was a dark apartment.

'One night there was a knocking at the door. No one was expected. He never had unexpected visitors. He turned off the television and the lights and stood in terror on the other side of the door. The only light came from under the door. He could see the shadow of someone standing in the hallway.

'The knocking came again. He could hardly breathe. Then there was the sound of paper being pushed under the door, and steps walking away.

'He waited a few minutes and then turned on the light. On the floor was an envelope, and in the envelope there was an unsigned Valentine card. . . .'

iv

Throughout the Bible, from the first verses of Genesis onward, darkness and light are posed against each other: 'In the beginning . . . darkness was upon the face of the deep . . . and God said, "Let there be light." ' John's gospel begins with its own Genesis verses: 'In him was life, and the life was the light of mankind. The light shines in the darkness and the darkness has not overcome it.' At Christmas, we re-read Isaiah's words: 'The people who walked in darkness have seen a great light, those who dwelt in a land of deep darkness, on them light was shined.'

Our ancestors in Isaiah's time lived in a dark world. Now it is nearly two thousand years since the birth of Jesus, yet our world is dark as well. Our darkness, like theirs, is our enmity: we are at odds with God, with others, with ourselves. We experience the darkness as anxiety, fear, loneliness and locked doors. We find ourselves all too ready to believe the worst of others, and easily forget their redeeming qualities.

On the other side of our locked door, there is someone standing in the light. Occasionally he delivers Valentine cards.

This small book does not argue that there is nothing to fear in this world, that there is no need for locks. There is a great deal to fear. Fear is reasonable. Our darkness is reasonable. Our enmity is reasonable. Our locks and weapons can all be explained rationally. We may all die of reasonably made decisions that launch a plague of nuclear missiles, all planned and designed by the most rational people on earth.

In these pages you will find an invitation to take the risk of love, to let your life be transformed by God's love. One of God's gifts to us, should we accept it, is encouragement, which is simply the gift of courage, courage to open the door, courage to live in a peaceful way even in dangerous times and places. (And what does courage mean? It simply means heart.)

At Cana, in Galilee, Jesus turned water into wine. He can also turn darkness into light, frightened hearts into courageous hearts, violent hands into healing hands, broken community into reconciled community. For the great miracle of Jesus is not turning water into wine but turning enmity into love.

Jim Forest

Acknowledgements

My gratitude goes to Yehezkel Landau, William Klassen and Landrum Bolling, who made it possible for me to spend a three-month sabbatical teaching and studying in Jerusalem at the Ecumenical Institute for Theological Research, Tantur; this book began as a Tantur lecture. Thanks also to those who encouraged me to let the lecture keep growing, especially Nancy, my wife; Rosemary Lynch, my teaching colleague at Tantur; Debbie Thorpe, my publisher at Marshall Pickering, who proposed the book and has helped bring it to completion; Siân Lloyd Jones, who edited the text; Françoise Pottier, my co-worker on the staff of the International Fellowship of Reconciliation and a constant source of inspiration; William Shannon, biblical scholar, editor of the letters of Thomas Merton, and friend; and Len Munnik, who did the drawings and whose sense of humour is one of the glories of Holland.

I am also grateful to the editors of the publications in which parts of this book first appeared and who have permitted re-publication: *Reconciliation International, Fellowship, Sojourners, The Other Side, Grass Roots, One World,* and the *1984–1985 Yearbook of the Ecumenical Institute for Theological Research.*

JF

'If only it were' all so simple!
If only there were evil people somewhere
insidiously committing evil deeds
and it were necessary only to separate them
from the rest of us and destroy them.
But the dividing line between good and evil
cuts through the heart of every human being,
and who is willing
to destroy a piece of his own heart?'

Alexander Solzhenitsyn
The Gulag Achipelago

Loving Enemies

1: Words carved on a Green Stick

Leo Tolstoy, as a child, was told by his older brother Nicholas that there was a green stick buried on the edge of a ravine in the ancient Zakaz forest in the heart of Russia. It was no ordinary piece of wood. Carved into its surface were words 'which would destroy all evil in the hearts of men and bring them everything good.' Tolstoy spent his entire life searching for the revelation of the green stick. As an old man he wrote, 'I still believe today that there is such a truth . . .'

The green stick, were we to discover it, would probably provide a text that has been read before. I believe it would reveal a few words that we have heard again and again but have buried on the edge of a remote ravine within ourselves: *'Love your enemies.'*

Twice in the gospels Jesus is quoted on this remarkable teaching:

> Love your enemies, do good to those who hate you, bless those who curse you, pray for those who abuse you. To him who strikes you on the cheek, offer the other also; and to him who takes away your cloak, do not withhold your coat as well. Give to everyone who begs from you; and of him who takes away your goods, do not ask them again. As you wish that others would do to you, do so to them. (Luke 6:27–31)

> You have heard that it was said, You shall love your neighbour and hate your enemy. But I say to you, Love your enemies and pray for those who persecute you, so that you may be children of your Father who is in

heaven; for he makes his sun rise on the evil and on the good, and sends rain on the just and on the unjust. For if you love those who love you, what reward have you? Do not even tax collectors do the same? (Matt 5:43–46)

Perhaps we have heard these words too often for them to surprise us, or perhaps they have been too elegantly translated for us to be stunned by the plain meaning. But to those who first heard Jesus speaking, this teaching must have been astonishing. Agreement would not have been easy. Some would have shrugged their shoulders and muttered, 'A Jew, love a Roman soldier? Ridiculous!' Zealots in the crowd would have considered such teaching traitorous, for enmity is the shadow side of nationalism. Speaking against enmity is to make enemies on the spot. Small wonder that, not long after he spoke these words, Jesus was condemned to death.

We tend to forget that the country in which Jesus entered history and gathered his first disciples was not the idyllic place Sunday school books have made of it. It was a country enduring military occupation in which anyone perceived as a dissident was likely to be executed. A Jew dying on the cross was not an unfamiliar sight. To Jesus' first audience, enemies were numerous, vicious and close at hand.

For the Jews, first of all there were the Romans to hate, with their armies and idols. Then there were tax collectors who extorted as much money as they could, for their own pay was a percentage of the take. There were the enemies within: Jews who were aping the Romans and Greeks, dressing — and undressing — as they did, all the while scrambling up the ladder, actively collaborating with the Roman occupiers. And even among those religious Jews trying to remain faithful to the tradition, there were divisions about what was and was not essential in religious law and practice, and there were sharp political divisions about how to relate to the Romans. A growing number of Jews — the Zealots — saw no solution but assassination and armed struggle. Some others — the Essenes — chose the strategy of monastic withdrawal; they lived in the desert near the Dead Sea where neither the Romans nor their collaborators often ventured.

Jesus also had Romans listening, some out of curiosity, others because it was their job to listen. From the Roman point of view, the indigestible Jews, even if momentarily subdued, still remained enemies. The Romans viewed this one-godded, statue-smashing, civilization-resisting people with amusement, bewilderment and contempt: a people well deserving whatever lashes they received. Some of those lashes would have been delivered by the Romans in blind rage at having been stationed in this appalling, uncultured backwater. Judaea and Galilee were not sought-after posts for Roman soldiers or diplomats.

Had we lived in Judaea or Galilee, would we have wanted to be identified with Jesus?

We know many did identify with him, indeed flocked to him, most of all the marginal people, the sick and those considered good-for-nothing. He loved sinners, the gospel says plainly; he loved them not just for *what* they might become but for *what* they were already. He came not for the well and the successful people but for the sick and the failures, but still there were others who came to him whose brokeness was less visible: scholars, soldiers, ordinary working people, respected and secure people, people who had a lot to lose. They too were drawn by his readiness to forgive, his ability to heal, his common sense, his utter truthfulness. They were drawn by his love, a love which included even them.

Perhaps there were those who were drawn by his grief. He was not a hard-hearted or complacent man, nor did he perform his wonders with a magician's detachment. The gospel records two occasions when Jesus wept in public — before the tomb of his dead friend Lazarus; and again as he approached Jeruselem on that final pilgrimage. It was while looking at Jerusalem, after his tears subsided, that he said, 'If only you knew the things which make for peace!' (Luke 19:41)

His capacity for grief was coupled with courage. Jesus was no coward. If he refused to take up weapons or bless their use, he kept no 'prudent silence', and he was anything but a collaborator. He did not hesitate to say and do things which made him a target. Perhaps the event that assured his crucifixion was what he did to the money changers working within the Temple precincts. He made a whip of cords (something which stings but causes no injury) and set the bankers running, overturning their tables and scattering their coins.

To say the least, not everyone was drawn to him. He was a man with many enemies. Some of them he acquired simply by being born a Jew and living where he lived. Others were more personal enemies, people whose animosity came in response to things he said or did. There were devout people who were shocked by his teaching and by what must have seemed careless religious practice. Some found it scandalous that he befriended all the wrong people, prostitues at the bottom of society; tax collectors and Roman officers at the top. We can assume the Zealots hated him both for not being a Zealot and for drawing away people who might have been recruited. Those who collaborated with the Romans were even more incensed. They actually managed to arrange his execution, pointing out to the Romans that Jesus was a trouble-maker, 'perverting the nation', (Luke 23:2) It was the Romans who, quite willingly, both tortured him and did the killing.

An orthodox Christian, believing Jesus to be God incarnate, entering history not by chance but purposefully and at an exact and chosen moment, will find it worthwhile to think about the Incarnation happening just then, in a humiliated, over-taxed land under military domination and kept within the empire by bitterly resented occupation troops. Jesus was born, lived, crucified and raised from the dead in a land of extreme enmity.

If we who live in the countries of the NATO alliance were to translate New Testament events into our time and place, we could say Jesus was born in a country where the

West's cold-war nightmare had come true: the Russians landing and taking command. Envisioning gospel events occurring today in our own world, quite possibly we would find ourselves dismayed or even appalled by the things Jesus did, and did not do; for actions that seem charming in an ancient tale might be judged unwise and untimely, if not insane, if they occurred here and now. Some would say he was useful to the nation's enemies; others that he had no one to blame for his troubles but himself.

Certainly Jesus is nothing like the popular male heroes of our century. He never wore a soldier's uniform or used a soldier's tools. He received no medals for valour under fire. He was not drawn into the front (or even rear) ranks of the nationalists and the armed resistance. He never killed anyone. His fame was for healing, even healing the wound of a man injured by a disciple who was only trying to defend Jesus from his enemies.

2: Who is my enemy?

The words enemy and enmity come from the Latin, *inimicus*, simply meaning someone who is not a friend.

My son Daniel, when he was seven, offered a very crisp definition of what it is to be a non-friend when he told another boy to 'go away and drop dead'. An enemy is someone, anyone, who would do well to go away and drop dead.

The *Oxford English Dictionary* gives a more elegant definition. An enemy, it says, is an 'unfriendly or hostile person, one that cherishes hatred, and who works to do ill to another.'

This is an astute entry, as it points the finger not only toward some distant person or nation but at oneself. We are used to perceiving others as enemies, never ourselves. But if *I* am unfriendly or hostile toward others, if *I* cherish hatred or participate in doing ill to others, or even if I am busy threatening or preparing to do ill, *I* am an enemy. The enemy of my enemy is me.

In this case who isn't an enemy? An American cartoon character, Pogo, whose home was a Florida swamp, used to say, 'We have met the enemy and he is us.'

An enemy is anyone I feel threatened by and seek to defend myself against. It is a person, or group of people, whose defeat I would count a gain. What for them would be bad news, for me would be good news. An ememy is someone whose death I would not mourn and might warmly welcome.

There are both domestic enemies and foreign ones. Very often one's chief enemy is someone very close at hand: a member of my family, a co-worker, a neighbour. Most crimes, including crimes of violence, occur either within the family or among friends. The courts are full of domestic cases. But domestic enemies may be people I don't know as individuals: blacks, Asians, gays, punks, pro-abortionists (or pro-lifers), people in expensive cars, people who dress in a certain way, people in particular religious groups. They may be people in political groups in oppostion to my own. They may be particular people in important roles of political leadership.

Internationally, an enemy is a mass of people I am encouraged to perceive as a threat and may, in case of war, be required to kill. Such enemies are not acquired through personal animosity but simply by birth and nationality. Such enmity seems to have a remarkably impersonal dimension, and in fact a former mortal enemy can abruptly become this year's trusted ally. The enemy is not an individual but a system, a party, or an entire people. For the Jews 2,000 years ago, the principal enemy was Rome, whose army occupied their land. For Americans 45 years ago, the principal enemies were Germany, Italy and Japan (today all allies), while today the enemy is the Soviet Union (at that time an ally). We in the West are collectively prepared for war with Russians, and Russians prepared for war with us. Given the inter-connectedness of the world, everyone, in various ways, participates in this enmity and suffers its consequences, no matter what their personal views are.

Political speeches, news items, cold-war movies and spy fiction all serve to develop and reinforce enemy stereotypes so that little by little one comes to regard an entire nation as an appropriate target of destruction. A fortune beyond the reach of imagination is expended in preparations for the destruction not merely of particular rulers with whom we are at odds, but everyone who lives under their rule. Actually, the rulers are the only ones who are likely to survive — in their concrete mansions deep underground.

3: What does it mean to love?

In modern usage love has mainly to do with good fortune in romance and sex. Love, says the *American Heritage Dictionary*, is 'intense affection and warm feeling for another person; strong sexual desire for another person; a strong fondness or enthusiasm; or a zero score in tennis.' Such a definition makes the commandment to love one's enemies incomprehensible. We can safely say that even Jesus was without intense affection or warm feelings for his judges, torturers and executioners.

The *Oxford English Dictionary* is both less emotional and more biblical: 'Love . . . [is that] disposition or state of feeling with regard to a person which . . . manifests itself in solicitude for the welfare of the object . . . [love is] applied in an eminent sense to the paternal benevolence and affection of God toward His children, to the affectionate devotion directed to God from His creatures, and to the affection of one created being to another so far as it is prompted by the sense of their common relationship to God.'

As used in the Bible, love has first of all to do with action and responsibility: the stress is not at all upon how one feels at the time. To love is to do what you can to provide for the wellbeing of another whether you like that person or not. What Jesus *does* is love. In explaining his Father's love, he talks about what God gives.

An act of love may be animated by a sense of gratitude and delight in someone else — wonderful when it happens — or it may be done despite anger, exhaustion, depression, fear or aversion, done simply as a prayer to God and a response to God, who links us all, who is our common Creator, our Father, our Mother, in whom we are brothers and sisters, 'who makes the sun rise on the evil and on the good, and sends rain on the just and the unjust', and who has bound together love of God with love of neighbour.

Paul believed that the greatest gifts of God were three-fold — faith, hope and love, and, of these, the greatest gift is love. Genuine love is patient and kind, without jealousy or boasting, without arrogance or rudeness: it does not demand its own way, does not rejoice at wrong but rather in right, and endures everything. (Cor. 13:4–7) In his love, Paul wrote to the church in Corinth, Jesus has reconciled us to himself and made us into 'ambassadors of Christ' called to undertake 'the ministry of reconciliation'. (2 Cor. 5:17–20)

Love is linked with reconciliation, but reconciliation is a word rarely used and often misunderstood. For some it means making a private peace with what is wrong in the world, accepting the status quo, smoothing over differences, and being friendly at all costs.

But the biblical meaning of reconciliation has to do with relationships that are transformed in the peace of God. Reconciliation means the restoration of community that has broken and seems beyond repair. Reconciliation is the healing of our deepest wounds. Events of reconciliation mark the way toward 'the Holy Mountain' of Isaiah's prophecy where 'the lion and the lamb shall dwell together . . . and a little child shall lead them.' (Isaiah 11:1–9)

Reconciliation was the great dream of Martin Luther King: 'I have a dream that one day on the red hills of Georgia, sons of former slaves and sons of former slave-owners will be able to sit down together at the table of brotherhood . . . I have a dream today!'[1]

Reconciliation is not only a word describing what *will* be, but also a reality that already exists. Even now, in all our fractured and broken relationships, we are profoundly inter connected and interdependent. None of us could live without the help of countless others. Everything we have, not only material things, but our words, our ideas, our skills, our faith, the music and stories which give courage and understanding and which delight the heart — everything we have has been given to us by others. 'We are already one,' said Thomas Merton a few weeks before his death, 'but we imagine that we are not. What we have to recover is our original unity.'[2]

4: The parable of the merciful enemy

One day Jesus was asked by a lawyer, 'What must I do to inherit eternal life?' (Luke 10:25)

Jesus thought this was something that any Jew should be able to answer, certainly a lawyer. 'What is written in the law?' Jesus asked. 'How do you read it?'

The lawyer replied, 'You shall love the Lord your God with all your heart, and with all your soul, and with all your strength, and with all your mind; and your neighbour as yourself.'

'You have answered right,' Jesus told him. 'Do this, and you will live.'

Then came the lawyer's real question: 'And who is my neighbour?'

Jesus then tells one of the gospel's most memorable parables. It is about a man walking along that desolate road that leads from the heights of Jerusalem down to Jericho. The man — perhaps it was Jesus himself — is attacked, beaten, and everything is taken, even his clothing. His assailants leave him bleeding, half-dead.

You know what followed: A priest and a Levite, two religiously employed fellow Jews, passed by the injured man 'on the other side of the road'. We can almost hear them talking later on about how dangerous it is to travel, even with all these Roman soldiers around.

Then a Samaritan came by. The Samaritans were those despised cousins of the Jews who had forsaken the holy city, Jerusalem. Though they, too, were committed to the law received by Moses, they were regarded as enemies in Judaea. But this nameless Samaritan, passing by, saw the injured man, 'had compassion on him, and went to him and bound up his wounds, pouring on oil and wine'. The Samaritan put the stranger on his donkey and took him to an inn where he paid the innkeeper to do everything he could for the man he had found dying on the road.

Jesus answered the lawyer's question with a story about how three people responded to a man in need. Two of them were, in a formal sense, neighbours to the man in the ditch. One of them, far from being a neighbour, was an enemy. But it was the enemy who set aside his plans, inconvenienced himself, spent his money, and committed himself to saving the life of someone who he had never met and who probably would not have wanted to meet him. It was the enemy who had compassion.

Jesus asks the lawyer, 'Which of the three, do you think, proved neighbour to the man who fell among robbers?'

The lawyer said, 'The one who showed mercy on him.'

And Jesus said, 'Go and do likewise.'

Are Christians more likely to respond to needy strangers? It seems not. Twenty years ago, at an American theological seminary, a number of students were asked to prepare sermons on the Parable of the Good Samaritan. These were not to be publicly delivered but simply put on tape for grading by a professor of homiletics. It seemed a rather ordinary seminary assignment, but those responsible for the project were more interested in this particular parable than any of the students realized. Unknown to the students, they had been arbitrarily divided into three groups: some were to be called on a certain morning and told that they could come to the taping room any time in the day; others were to be told that they had to be there within the next few hours; and the rest were to be told that they had to come without delay.

The testers had arranged that, as each student arrived at the building where the sermons were being recorded, they would find someone lying on the ground by a bench near the entrance.

What were the results? Among all those preaching sermons on the Parable of the Good Samaritan, barely a third took the time to stop and do anything for the person lying on the ground. Those who did stop, it was discovered, were mainly the ones who felt they had time. They weren't struggling with deadlines and overcrowded schedules — the constant problem of those in the ministry, which perhaps is why Jesus cast a priest and Levite in those unfortunate parts in his parable.

5: On the road to Emmaus

The sense of having time, or not having it, is not simply a matter of having a full or empty diary. Sometimes people who lead the most complicated lives manage to drop everything and respond to the unexpected as if there was nothing else that mattered. It is often in unplanned and perhaps unwanted events that God breaks open our lives.

I think of Rosemary Lynch, a Franciscan nun nearing seventy but with the energy of a fifteen-year-old. She lives in Las Vegas, Nevada — not the tourist part with bright lights and gambling casinos, but in the black neighbourhood where there aren't even street lights. From time to time, her small Franciscan community takes responsibility for newly arrived refugees, who may come from Central America, Vietnam or, occasionally, from eastern Europe.

One of the refugees Rosemary's community received was a Russian woman who was a professional restorer of icons. There is no demand, however, for icon restoration in Las Vegas. Finally the sisters found her a job clearing tables in the restaurant of a gambling casino.

One night she returned from her job in tears, hardly able to speak. 'I cannot continue this work,' she explained while still crying. 'They make me throw away the body of Jesus.'

'What do you mean?' the sisters asked in astonishment.

'The bread, the body of Jesus. If there is any bread left on the table, even if no one touched it, you have to throw it away. No one else can have it. You have to throw away the body of Jesus.'

The sisters assured their guest that they would help her find a different job and thanked her that she had given them the traditional Russian awareness that *all* bread is a sign of the presence of Jesus and not only bread consecrated on the altar.

For some years I was part of the Emmaus community in New York's East Harlem, a house of hospitality for runaways and ex-prisoners; it could also have been called a house of bread for strangers; and certainly it was a house of interruptions. We had many guests. Not only was every bed filled at night, but people often slept on the living-room floor. We always had too much to do.

One day a visiting artist drew a picture of sliced bread on our living room wall and, in huge letters, wrote the Emmaus story from Luke's gospel around the bread. We read it often, until any of us could have recited it by heart.

We developed a deep sense of identification with the two disciples in Luke's story. For them, it seemed that everything important in life had been destroyed with Jesus' death. Then, as they were walking from Jerusalem to Emmaus, they met a stranger:

While they were talking and discussing together, Jesus himself drew near and went with them, but their eyes were kept from recognizing him. And he said to them, 'What is this conversation which you are holding with each other as you walk?' And they stood still, looking sad. One of them, named Cleopas, answered him. 'Are you the only visitor in Jerusalem who does not know the things that have happened there in these days?' And he said to them, 'What things?'

The disciples told him how Jesus, who seemed to be a mighty prophet and whom they had hoped would redeem Israel, had been crucifed. They also told him that 'some women of our company' claimed that Jesus had been raised from the dead, but they had actually gone to the burial place and found no sign of a revived Jesus, only an empty tomb.

Jesus then spoke to them at length, 'interpreting to them everything in the scripture concerning himself, beginning with Moses and going on to all the prophets'. His narrative continued until they found themselves entering the village of Emmaus.

> Jesus appeared to be going further, but they constrained him, saying, 'Stay with us, for it is toward evening and the day is now far spent.' So he went to stay with them. When he was at table with them, he took the bread and blessed it, and gave it to them. And their eyes were opened and they recognized him, and he vanished out of their sight. They said to each other, 'Did not our hearts burn within us while he talked to us on the road, while he opened to us the scriptures?' And they rose that same hour and returned to Jerusalem where they found the eleven gathered together and those who were with them, who said, 'The Lord is risen indeed and has appeared to Simon!' Then they told what had happened on the road, and how they knew him in the breaking of bread. (Luke 24:12–35)

Their encounter with Jesus began while they were in a state of shock and sorrow. What sorrow it is to discover someone who means so much to you is not the person you had thought. You discover, for example, that someone whose songs or writing have shifted the foundations of your life, who has helped shape your faith and your vocation, is actually a vain and superficial person. His great subject may be God, but in person his great subject is himself. The discovery is deeply wounding. Our heroes are not as different from ourselves as we want them to be.

Certainly, the Messiah, the Anointed One, the Christ, was an immense disappointment to his disciples. He was very human. He had seemed to be a prophet 'mighty in deed and word before God and all the people' and yet he proved to be as vulnerable as any of Israel's countless dissenters, as easily made to bleed as any Jew. The religious leaders and secular overlords had condemned him to death and, without the intervention of angels, the sentence had been carried out with grim military efficiency.

'But we had hoped that he was the one to redeem Israel.' We had hoped that, through his mighty power, we would be liberated at last from our humiliators: soldiers, tax collectors, collaborators and executioners.

But now he is dead. Three days have passed and the world is unchanged, the executioners still in charge. The money changers have repaired their tables and it's business as usual both in the marketplace and the temple.

The stranger on the road seemed to be such a fool. He seemed not to know what was going on. 'Are you the only one who hasn't heard?'

His response seemed even more tactless than their question. They were the foolish ones, he said. They didn't understand or believe the promises that had been handed down by the prophets since ancient times; promises that a wounded healer would be given to the world through Israel, a man whose bones would be crushed as if in the jaws of a lion, but who would open the way to the holy mountain where spears would be turned into ploughs, and no one would learn war anymore. (Isaiah 11:1-9)

The disciples neither believed the prophecies nor the resurrection testimony of those in their community who came running back from the empty tomb. The witnesses were women. 'Some women in our company amazed us.' In fact it had been mainly women who had been with Jesus when he was being executed; John was the only male disciple standing at the foot of the cross. It was women who had gone to the burial place and met angels.

Women were the first to believe in the risen Christ. The men could not. Mark also writes about this. Mary Magdalene, he says, actually saw Jesus (first thinking he was a gardener; only realizing the truth when he pronounced her name), and then she went to tell 'those who had been with him, as they mourned and wept . . . but they would not believe'. (Mark 16:10-11)

The two disciples on the road were among those who

didn't believe. They had decided to leave the city, broken-hearted refugees whose hopes had perished with Jesus' body, walking in such gloom that they had no idea who it was they met on the road. Nor had it occurred to them to invite him to join with them as they walked.

Uninvited, unwelcomed, the stranger had attached himself to them. But when they reached Emmaus, it was they who pressed him to stay. Thus it was they who initiated the time — having no idea of the revelation they were about to experience — of Eucharist; the encounter with Jesus in bread and wine.

On the road, 'their eyes were kept from recognizing him.' But at the table in Emmaus, they were given a kind of sight they had never known before in their lives. 'He took bread and blessed it, and broke it, and gave it to them. And their eyes were opened and they recognized him . . . they knew him in the breaking of bread.'

No doubt it was only when he was holding the bread in his hands that they noticed the wounds.

Then 'he vanished out of their sight.' One imagines a magician's trick, like a disappearing rabbit, but perhaps they were blinded by their own tears, tears of joy, of gratitude. When they recovered, he was gone.

They did not search for him, for there was no need to bring him back to the table: he had left himself on the table in the bread. That was clear to them, as it has been clear to Christians ever since. Jesus is no further away from our lives than bread. We know him 'in the breaking of bread.'

At Emmaus House, where we daily broke bread with strangers, we learned the simplest truth of faith, the truth at the heart of this resurrection narrative: the Christian life is the continual rediscovery of the face of Jesus in those around us. Suddenly, often when we least expect it, a word is said, an expression alters an unexplored face, we glimpse joy or beauty in someone we regarded with irritation or contempt, and the idea we had had of that other person is demolished. We find ourselves in the presence of a huge mystery. That face had seemed so easily mapped, so safely flat, a kind of dull wallpaper. Yet suddenly a seam is revealed, a door swings opens, and we are in Christ's presence.

6: Fourth and walnut

It is often hard enough to detect Christ's presence in those who are attractive, similar to ourselves, neighbours, best friends, members of our own family and household, participants in some of the best moments in our lives. What can open our eyes to those who are unattractive, culturally different, irritating, even dangerous or perceived (rightly or wrongly) as mortal enemies? How can one speak of loving those who fill us with anxiety or revulsion? Can one just decide to love, in the way one might decide to learn a language or climb a mountain?

In fact love is always possible with God's help. But we block that help with obstacles within ourselves which commit us to enmity — pride, contempt, prejudice, racism, selfishness, the vice of our own plans and ambitions or entrapment in group ambition and nationalism which makes one portion of the human race of more worth than another.

The obstacles within ourselves often seem impossible to overcome. I think of the author, Thomas Merton, my friend during the last seven years of his life. He was a brilliant man who had received his education in France, England and America. He possessed a marvellous sense of humour, but its dark side was ruthless sarcasm. His tendency to look down on others had been little changed by his conversion to Christianity, his entrance into the Catholic Church, or his becoming a member of a Trappist monastic community. His writings chronicle the conversion of a profoundly secular intellectual to Christianity, then follow his development from an intensely parochial form of Catholicism to profound awareness of the activity of God in other Christian churches, then in non-Christian religions, and finally in every corner of life. Though nearly twenty years have passed since his death, his books continue to be widely read in many countries.

He had been a monk for many years when one of the turning points in his life occurred, an intense experience of God's presence in others and God's love for them — people whom Merton normally regarded with profound condescension. It happened when he had occasion to be in the city closest to the Abbey of Gethsemani.

In Louisville, at the corner of Fourth and Walnut, in the centre of the shopping district, I was suddenly over-whelmed by the realization that I loved all those people, that they were mine and I theirs, that we could not be alien to one another even though we were total strangers. It was like waking from a dream of separateness, of spurious self-isolation in a special world, the world of renunciation and supposed holiness. The whole illusion of a separate holy existence is a dream . . . This sense of liberation from an illusory difference was such a relief and such a joy to me that I almost laughted out loud . . . It is a glorious destiny to be a member of the human race, though it is a race dedicated to many absurdities and one which makes many terrible mistakes: yet, with all that, God Himself gloried in becoming a member of the human race. A member of the human race! To think that such a commonplace realization should suddenly seem like news that one holds the winning ticket in a cosmic sweepstake . . . There is no way of telling people that they are all walking around shining like the sun . . . There are no strangers . . . If only we could see each other [as we really are] all the time. There would be no more war, no more hatred, no more cruelty, no more greed . . . I suppose the big problem is that we would fall down and worship each other . . . the gate of heaven is everywhere.[3]

In that moment, Merton had a illuminating experience of the truth: that we are, each of us, made in the image and likeness of God. For a moment he saw with God's eyes the strangers around him, and knew God's measureless love for each of us.

For Merton, this experience helped him to see himself and his vocation in an entirely new light, without the burden of disdain for others. He realized that a religious community is not an 'escape from the world' but rather a place of the deepest engagement 'in the struggles and sufferings of the world'.[4]

Before his moment of grace at Fourth and Walnut, Merton had maintained few contacts with people outside the monastery; during the years that followed, he developed an immense network of friendships, mainly carried on by letter, which stretched around the world. It came to include an amazing diversity of people: popes, Zen masters, teachers of Islam, Russian novelists, Latin American poets, prisoners, scientists, even high school students. He also began a deep engagement with the peace movement, especially the Catholic Worker, Pax Christi, the Catholic Peace Fellowship, and the Fellowship of Reconciliation.

One of the convictions which Merton came to in his later years, a truth he often returned to in letters and talks, was that Christianity is not about the love of ideas and principles, as it had once seemed to him, but the love of people. Love, Merton insisted, must grow to include even those who are radically different from ourselves, even those who threaten us: 'It is my belief' he wrote, 'that we should not be too sure of having found Christ until we have found Him in that part of humanity that is most remote from our own.'

Love must be strong enough to carry us into what may seem to be hopeless endeavours. As he put it in a letter he sent me at a rather dark time in my life, when it seemed nothing the peace movement was doing was stopping or even slowing the awful destruction going on in Vietnam:

Do not depend on the hope of results. When you are doing . . . an apostolic work [such as work for peace], you may have to face the fact that your work will be apparently worthless and even achieve no result at all, if not perhaps results opposite to what you expect. As you get used to this idea, you start more and more to concentrate not on the results but on the value, the rightness, the truth of the work itself. And there too a great deal has to be gone through, as gradually you struggle less for an idea and more and more for specific people. The range tends to narrow down, but it gets much more real. *In the end, it is the reality of personal relationships that saves everything.*

. . . I am, to tell the truth, nauseated by ideals and with causes. This sounds like heresy, but I think you will understand what I mean. It is so easy to get engrossed with ideas and slogans and myths that in the end one is left holding the bag, empty, with no trace of meaning left in it. And then the temptation is to yell louder than ever in order to make the meaning be there again by magic . . .

The big results are not in your hands or mine, but they suddenly happen, and we can share in them; but there is no point in building our lives on this personal satisfaction, which may be denied to us and which after all is not that important . . .

The great thing, after all, is to live, not to pour out your life in the service of a myth: and we turn the best things into myths. If you can get free from the domination of causes and just service Christ's truth, you will be able to do more and will be less crushed by the inevitable disappointments . . .

The real hope . . . is not in something we think we can do, but in God who is making something good out of it in some way we cannot see. If we can do His will, we will be helping in the process. But we will not necessarily know all about it beforehand.[5] (italics added)

'In the end it is the reality of personal relationships that saves everything.' This is another way of saying that God is with us, and not in a vague sense, like a slogan or a flag. This is what the Incarnation, God sharing our own flesh, is all about: everyone is knit together in personal relationships. God is present now and not only in a past inhabited by our long-dead ancestors. God, who is life itself, is with us in life, so that nothing is insignificant. As Jesus said: 'I came that they may have life, and have it abundantly.' (John 10:10)

It is because of his presence, here and now, that we can dare to think of any kind of miracles and transformation in our own lives and in the way human beings live together.

7: Water into wine

In the Lady Chapel of London's Westminster Cathedral there is a mosaic which tells the story of the miracle at Cana in one simple image: a man is pouring water from one large jug into another; the water leaves the first jug a light, sparkling blue and becomes a deep purple before it reaches the lip of the lower jug. Before our eyes, water turns to wine.

> This, the first of his signs, Jesus did at Cana, in Galilee, and manifested his glory; and his disciples believed in him. (John 2:11)

Until noticing this mosaic, it had never occurred to me that this 'first sign' that Jesus gave — a miracle of transformation — is a key to understanding everything in the gospel. Jesus is constantly involved in transformation: water into wine, bread and wine into himself, blind eyes to seeing eyes, withered limbs to working limbs, guilt into forgiveness, strangers into neighbours, enemies into friends, slaves into free people, dead bodies into living bodies, crucifixion into resurrection, sorrow into joy. Nature cannot grow figs from thistles, but God is doing this in our lives all the time. God's constant business in creation is making something out of nothing. As the Portuguese say, 'God writes straight with crooked lines.'

The word *grace* is often used to describe the way God enters into our lives. We can speak of 'graced moments' when we see another person in such a way that we realize that, until that moment, we were blind. We 'saw' but in such a dark, superficial way that we were unaware of God's presence in that other life. These moments when God breaks through in us are the main events in our lives. Invariably they are turning points; we are changed. These are moments of unspeakable happiness. For the rest of our lives we know that what the poet Leon Bloy said is utterly true: 'Joy is the most infallible sign of the presence of God.'

Yevgeny Yevtushenko, one of the most loved Russian poets, is notable for his description of transforming moments. Sometimes these have to do with compassion taking the place of enmity. It is a remarkable theme when you begin to understand what Russians of his generation experienced — Stalin on the one hand, Hitler on the other, and both tearing millions of lives to shreds. It was only in reading his autobiography that I began to understand what makes this theme so central to his writing. One story especially stood out.

In 1944, Yevtushenko's mother took him from Siberia to Moscow. They were among those who witnessed a procession of twenty thousand German war prisoners marching through the streets of Moscow:

The pavements swarmed with onlookers, cordoned off by soldiers and police. The crowd was mostly women — Russian women with hands roughened by hard work, lips untouched by lipstick, and with thin hunched shoulders which had borne half of the burden of the war. Every one of them must have had a father or a husband, a brother or a son killed by the Germans. They gazed with hatred in the direction from which the column was to appear.

At last we saw it. The generals marched at the head, massive chins stuck out, lips folded disdainfully, their whole demeanour meant to show superiority over their plebian victors.

'They smell of perfume, the bastards,' someone in the crowd said with hatred. The women were clenching their fists. The soldiers and policemen had all they could do to hold them back.

All at once something happened to them. They saw German soldiers, thin, unshaven, wearing dirty, blood-stained bandages, hobbling on crutches or leaning on the shoulders of their comrades; the soldiers walked with their heads down. The street became dead silent — the only sound was the shuffling of boots and the thumping of crutches.

Then I saw an elderly women in broken-down boots push herself forward and touch a policeman's shoulder, saying, 'Let me through'. There must have been something about her that made him step aside. She went up to the column, took from inside her coat something wrapped in a coloured handkerchief and unfolded it. It was a crust of black bread. She pushed it awkwardly into the pocket of a soldier, so exhausted that he was tottering on his feet. And now from every side women were running toward the soldiers, pushing into their hands bread, cigarettes, whatever they had. The soldiers were no longer enemies. They were people.[6]

It is a story of a Cana-like miracle, except in this case it is not water but vinegar that is changed to wine.

8: Living in the night of fear

Once a rabbi asked his students, 'When can we know that the night has ended and the day begun?'

'Is it the moment,' suggested one student, 'when you can tell the difference between a sheep and a dog?'

'No,' said the rabbi.

'Is it,' asked another, 'when you can see the difference between a fig tree and an olive tree?'

'Not that either,' said the rabbi.

'Then when is it?' the students asked. And the rabbi answered:

'It is the moment when you can look at a face never seen before and recognize the stranger as a brother or sister. Until that moment, no matter how bright the day, it is still the night.'

Most of us would have to admit that we are living in the night. Instead of seeing sisters and brothers, we see labels: white or black, male or female, straight or gay, left or right, friend or enemy. We come to know who to welcome and who to keep at a distance, who to care for and who to ignore. We become committed defenders of the night.

There is another story about daybreak occurring in the middle of the night:

And in that region there were shepherds out in the field, keeping watch over their flock by night. And an angel of the Lord appeared to them, and the glory of the Lord shone around them, and they were filled with fear. And the angel said to them, 'Be not afraid . . .' (Luke 2:8–10)

Hearing these familiar words, cheerful scenes spring to mind: quiet people in handsome robes gathered around a fire on a hillside, and winged angels dressed for a wedding floating in a sky full of stars, the brightest of which is suspended over the attractive town of Bethlehem.

A key word in Luke's narrative — fear — is easily passed over.

Luke writes about fear in the night; a fear soon set aside for joy by the birth the angel announces, but a birth that will stir the fear of Herod so profoundly that in the coming days his troops will murder the younger sons of Bethlehem.

The night that came over the shepherds was, of course, the night that exists between sunset and sunrise. But perhaps they too lived in that longer night, the night of fear and suspicion. They had much to fear.

For the people of Judea, it was not a Christmas-card world — no more than it is for us twenty centuries later. We, too, live in a world in which fear governs both major social events and private decisions. Fear is what enmity feels like. If the Jews were afraid of the Romans, many people in the NATO countries are afraid of the Russians (and some fear the Americans). The Russians, of course, are afraid of the Americans (and the Chinese, Poles, Hungarians, Czechs, Yugoslavs, and Afghans). Many people, in both east and west, are still afraid of the Germans (including some of the Germans). There are people in every country afraid of foreigners and refugees. There is fear of criminals (and often fear of the police). There is fear of the poisons we have released into the water and air, fear of technology that seems to spread with no social control and no awareness of social and environmental consequences. There is fear of joblessness, loss of home and possessions, loss of social significance. There is fear of illness and abandonment. There are large numbers of people afraid of war, even expecting to die in a forthcoming nuclear battle. There is fear of death and of the possibility that death opens into nothing, or into a fiery hell. Such is our dark night.

Into the night sky of the shepherds, an angel appeared.

Angels are very little mentioned in our day, perhaps little believed in, so we would probably be even more terrified than the shepherds were to see such a magnificent being.

Angels are frightening even for people who believe in them. Zachariah fell on the Temple floor in terror when the angel brought him the news of his wife's pregnancy; he was struck dumb. Joseph was frightened when the angel came to help him overcome his reluctance to marry Mary. Even Mary was frightened; to her, as to the others, the angel said, 'Be not afraid'. (Luke 1:30)

Nor was fear unknown to the disciples of Jesus. When Jesus walked on the water, when he was transfigured on Mount Tabor, and finally when he was raised from the dead, he had to tell them to set aside their fear. 'Do not be afraid. Go and tell my brethren to go to Galilee, and there they will see me.' (Mat.28:10)

Nicholas Berdyaev, a Marxist in the early days of the Russian revolution but later one of the great Christian theologians and contemplatives, took away from his encounter with Marxism a commitment to see things as they are rather than as one would like them to be, no matter how fearful the encounter with reality. 'It is the Christian duty,' he wrote, 'to look reality in the face and to keep ourselves fully conscious of it. Nothing is more unchristian than the "idealization" of reality; *it is precisely the Christian more than anybody else who must put aside fear whenever the exposure and condemnation of a horrible and wicked reality is called for.* . . . The human body must be seen naked to know its beauty, and in the same way Christianity demands that realities be stripped of their artificial adornments.'[7]

Thomas Merton had much in common with Berdyaev, including the constant struggle to see reality free of illusion. In his last years, Merton became more and more engaged in reflection on war and social disorder and attentive to the part fear plays in both our political and spiritual lives. In one of his essays he concluded that 'the root of war is fear'. It is 'not so much the fear men have of one another as the fear they have of *everything*. It is not that they do not trust one another, they do not even trust themselves.' Out of their fear, Merton argued, the human race has taken itself to the edge of self-extinction, and there are even Christians who see self-destruction as an act of God. An authentic Christianity must shake off fear and every notion of an incinerator god and commit itself 'to the total abolition of war' much as earlier Christians struggled for the abolition of slavery.[8]

A Marxist friend of mine who read Merton's essay at the time, responded, 'It's all right as far as it goes, and it is amazing to see a Christian writer even thinking critically about war, but actually the root of war is bad economic structures.' Some years later he wrote again to say, 'I keep thinking of what Merton said, and now I agree, because I realize that the root of bad economic structures is also fear.'

It is interesting to look at Jesus' life with special attention to the theme of fear. Even as a child, we find him daring to remain in Jerusalem in order to enter into discussion with teachers of the Law. Later we see him abandoning the securities of normal life to become a homeless person, a wandering teacher: 'The foxes have their holes and the birds their nests but the son of man has nowhere to lay his head.' (Matt. 8:20) Jesus has the courage to be with, even to be touched by, people in a legal condition of 'uncleanness': lepers, bleeding women, the dead. He is willing to be associated with despised people. Such associations imply his having overcome one of the strongest fears, the fear of condemnation and rejection by one's peers. He had the courage to turn over the moneytables in the Temple. He was without fear in his encounters with those who arrested him, judged him, tortured him and crucified him. Yet this fearless man is full of the fear of God.

Paradoxically, it is 'fear of God' that raises up the most fearless people. That holy fear is profound awareness of the power and majesty of God as creator and ruler of the universe, the God whom we must obey no matter what.

The *un*holy fear we are called away from both by the

angel and by Jesus is that fear which inspires cowardice,
makes us flee from conscience, blocks us from responding
to those around us, makes us insensitive to others, blinds
us in such a way that we fail to recognize that each of us
is made in the image and likeness of God, strips us of our
ability to recognize others as brothers and sisters.

These few words — *be not afraid* — are at the heart of
the gospel. Trapped in fear, we are powerless to be
disciples. There is very little we can do about the double
commandment: to love God, and to love each other.

Jesus is the great joy announced by the angel precisely
because he shows us that we do not have to centre our lives
on fear, fear of enemies or of all the other terrors life holds
for us or even fear of death. In offering us an example of
a life lived without fear, Jesus liberates us from a way of
life that is imprisoned in fear; not that we will never know
fear, but that fear will no longer take the place of God in
our lives.

It was not only to the shepherds but to ourselves that
the angel said, 'Be not afraid'.

9: Loving where love is impossible

'It's quite easy to say wonderful things about love, especially between wars,' a retired British army officer said to me over a meal. 'I don't mind being a vegetarian between meals. But you weren't even wearing your first nappies when people like me were faced with the Nazis, and bombs were falling on our houses. What would you have had us do? Drop Bibles on Germany?'

Not long after, at a small church meeting in Moscow, I met a Ukrainian Baptist. 'I am the sole survivor in my family,' he said in halting English. 'The only one. My parents, my grandparents, my sisters, my brothers, my cousins — all dead. You cannot imagine what the Nazis did. What could anyone do but fight back? What would you have done?'

I could only say I didn't know what I would have done. I was too small to know there was a war, though my father was among those in the army. How can one regard those who risked — and often lost — their lives fighting under arms against fascism, except with admiration? But the question that faces us is not what we would have done at some time in the past, nor is it to blame anyone, then or now, who sees no method of defence except through violence. The question is what can we do now and in the future to prevent another world war. There were many people in the last war whose active non-violent struggle against the Nazis may give us clues about alternatives to war in the future.

One of Hitler's unarmed opponents was Kasper Mayr. He is a former secretary of the International Fellowship of Reconciliation and the father of my colleague, Hildegard Goss-Mayr. The Mayr home, with its large garden and fruit trees, still stands on the outskirts of Vienna. As the Russian troops closed in on what had been one of the principal cities of the Third Reich, the citizens of Vienna — even those few, like Kasper Mayr, who had openly resisted the Nazis — had every reason for dread. Hitler's armies, to which many thousands of Austrians had belonged, caused twenty-million deaths in the USSR and destroyed most of Russia's industrial centres and western cities.

'Here was a victorious army,' Hildegard recalls, 'that would take revenge, that would rape its way to the centre of the city. In the face of these expectations, my father had closed the door to our house but did not lock it.' With his wife, daughter and some family guests in the cellar, he waited upstairs, no doubt in prayer. 'When the Russians approached and pounded against the door with their guns, father opened it and stood before them in a way they could not have expected. He pushed aside their rifles and gestured that they should come in, as if they were invited guests. Of course a soldier's attitude at such a moment is one of suspicion. He has seen six years of war and wants to survive. He is ready to shoot before he is shot. But they saw in my father's gesture that perhaps their fear was not necessary. They looked in the house to see if it was a trap. They found it wasn't. My father could see that they were relieved. They took off their rifles. And then my father called the others up from the basement. He was able to create an atmosphere of welcome, of trust, of love, of belonging.' Far from raping the women and killing any of the occupants of the house, the soldiers were moved to share their own meagre rations. 'They could see how thin and hungry we were — for the city had been cut off for quite some time. They shared with our family and guests from their own food.'

It was one of those moments when, if one lives by the Gospel According to Rambo, one relies on guns rather than unlocked doors and gestures of welcome. But as Hildegard points out, 'If father had used a weapon, he could not have protected those others in the house, who might have been raped and even killed. If my father had been armed, the Russian soldiers would have been confirmed in their fears. Instead, out of his inner strength and calm, he was able to affirm their humanity and to take them out of the terrible way of war. Nobody is an angel, and often war brings out the worst in people. My father's approach made it more likely to bring out the best, but of course you never know what will happen. Those soldiers might have acted violently no matter what my father did. Still, when you believe in the strength of truth and love, you must respond this way no matter what the danger is. You have to prefer to be killed yourself rather than to kill another.'

10: A city of refuge

Yes, you might say, there are moments when the individual manages to do something remarkable. But these are exceptional people; saints, not ordinary people.

But consider another story from the Hitler years. Le Chambon is a town in the mountains of southern France. Here 700 townspeople, and 2,000 peasants on outlying farms, together managed to save an estimated 10,000 Jews from the Holocaust. Inspired by the Mosaic dictate in Numbers 35:11, they made Le Chambon 'a city of refuge': a place of sanctuary for those in danger. In doing so, everyone in the village risked arrest, imprisonment and death. The danger was acute because life-saving work on such a scale simply could not be hidden. What they did was an act of collective heroism on an extraordinary scale, and yet those who did it were quite 'ordinary' people.[9]

The person who most inspired the villagers to risk so much was their pastor, André Trocmé, a devout Christian, passionate in his faith. He abhorred racism and hatred, and refused to have anything to do with war or killing. He was a determined and open opponent of fascism. One of his sons was among the villagers who died for their part in the village's action of non-violent resistance. Trocmé nearly paid with his life as well when, in the winter of 1943, he was arrested and taken away.

He was out visiting parishioners in remote farms when the police, after cutting telephone lines into Le Chambon and stationing guards at key locations around the town, arrived at his house. Hours passed. By the time Trocmé returned, the evening meal was ready. André's wife, Magda, insisted he be given time to eat, and then invited

the police to join the family at the table. Meanwhile seven
Jews were nervously in hiding in the attic.

The police presence at the Trocmé house was quickly
noticed by the villagers. Little by little they gathered
outside the presbytery to offer their farewells. When André
Trocmé stepped from the house, his neighbours embraced
their pastor and gave him packets containing precious gifts
in those times of extreme austerity: candles, warm socks,
toilet paper, chocolate, biscuits, a tin of sardines, even a
sausage. One of the officers said, 'I have never seen such
a farewell, never'. Like so many others at that moment, he
too was weeping. In his official report of the arrest, he
dared to say that the people of Le Chambon were 'full of
love'. As Trocmé was taken away, one woman began to sing
the hymn, 'A Mighty Fortress Is Our God'. In moments the
entire village, overcoming grief, was singing it with her.

Twice our family has gone as pilgrims to Le Chambon.
It is many years since André Trocmé's death, and still more
since he was pastor in that town, yet they still speak of
Pastor Trocmé's long walks through snow and rain to visit
the sick, and even today they remember his sermons.

'I especially remember his preaching about the Parable
of the Good Samaritan,' we were told by an old farmer.
'That story became the way we lived in those years. The
people we took in or helped across the Swiss border, these
people were ones who had been stripped and beaten and
left at the side of the road to die. How could we *not* open
our homes to such people? How could we say no to them
and call ourselves Christians? How could we even keep the
Bible in our house and not accept them too?'

It was one of the small miracles of the war that Trocmé
survived his imprisonment and lived on for many years.
Magda — now in her 80s — is still alive and still the sort
of person who wouldn't hesitate in inviting her enemies to
sit at the family table. It surprises her, in fact, that anyone
could imagine not feeding their enemies. 'They have to eat
too,' she says. 'And usually what they do is only because

they are afraid. They are afraid of what will happen to them if they say no.'

11: Reconciliation before communion

What is it that turns people toward killing?

Certainly there are those for whom it is a matter of deep conviction; many fought Hitler quite willingly, and many Germans and Austrians eagerly joined Hitler's armies. But for the majority, social compulsion is the decisive factor. Even the most popular wars have not been possible without conscription. Men are given the alternative of either submitting to military service or going into prison. A still more important factor for many men is the fear of being thought a coward. And there are many — I was one of them — who find military service an attractive first step away from home: travel, room and board, free medical care, and, at the same time, being on one's own at least some of the time. For some older men, military service gives the abandonment of an unpleasant domestic life a noble façade. There are also those eager for death-risking adventure and a licence to possess and use deadly weapons. And for everyone, propaganda plays a major role, for we are taught collectively to hate.

But what about killing done apart from war?

In *Crime and Punishment*, Dostoyevsky explores how aversion turns to hatred and hatred to murder. A brilliant student, Raskolnikov, in debt to a money-lender in St. Petersburg, spends long hours imagining how, through one act of violence, he might obtain a miserly old woman's fortune.

One can say Raskolnikov becomes a disciple of St. Napoleon. He thinks about Napoleon, whose 'greatness' freed him from the burden of 'ordinary' morality: how in the name of national glory, he was able to kill without limit and yet no-one called him a murderer. Napoleon 'destroys Toulon, butchers Paris, forgets an army in Egypt, expends half a million men in the Moscow campaign, shakes himself free with a pun in Vilno, and when he is dead, they put up monuments to him.' Was not Raskolnikov as free as Napoleon to take a life?

At last he commits his murder, in fact two, but only after he has provided — even published — a philosophical justification for ignoring morality.

In Dostoyevsky's scrutiny of the intellectual and spiritual life of Raskolnikov in the months preceding the actual killing, the reader is invited to realize that Raskolnikov is a murderer even while his victim is still alive and well. Within himself Raskolnikov has crossed the border into hell. Yet he perceives himself not as a murderer but as a man above normal limits: he is an intellectual; he has purposes which transcend the ordinary; what he is doing will ultimately be 'salutary to mankind'. And what right, anyway, does such an old woman have to life when she sits on a hoard of money that he can use in so many excellent ways?

For Dostoyevsky, Raskolnikov is not an exceptional person, but rather a heightened image of modern man and woman, desperate to possess and control, enslaved by money, in a state of alienation from each other and from God. Dostoyevsky sees Raskilnikov as the inevitable product of a world fouled by atheism, the word meaning not simply an ideology of disbelief but a basic godlessness, one form of which may actually be hidden beneath a veneer of socially conformed religion. What can one say of 'believers' who have no awe of creation, who are ready to kill, and even write theological justifications for killing?

Dostoyevsky's insight is not new. In the Sermon on the Mount, Jesus reminds his listeners of the prohibition of killing in the Ten Commandments.

But I say to you that everyone who is angry with his

brother shall be liable to judgement . . . and whoever says. 'You fool!' shall be liable to the fire of hell. (Matt. 5:21–22)

Jesus is concerned not only with acts of deadly violence but with the psychological and spiritual events that precede killing.

So fundamental is respect for the lives of others in the teaching of Jesus that he sees worship as incompatible with enmity. In the same portion of the Sermon on the Mount, he says:

So, if you are offering your gift at the altar and there remember that your brother has something against you, leave your gift there before the altar and go; first be reconciled with your brother, and then come and offer your gift. (Matt. 5:23,24)

In the communal worship of the early church, one of the main actions of the Mass of the Catechumens (those coming into the church but not yet invited to participate in communion) was the exchange of the kiss of peace. Vestiges of this rite still survive in many churches. The ritual reflects the church's understanding that Jesus' followers must be a people at peace both with one another and with their enemies.

The great second century theologian, Clement of Alexandria, was an exceptional writer and preacher, but was unexceptional in his teaching of unarmed discipleship. He defined the church as 'an army which sheds no blood':

Now the trumpet sounds with a mighty voice calling the soldiers of the world to arms, announcing war. And shall not Christ, who has uttered his summons to peace even to the ends of the earth, summon together his own soldiers of peace? Indeed, O Man, he has called to arms with his Blood and his Word an army that sheds no blood. To these soldiers he has handed over the Kingdom

of Heaven . . . Let us be armed for peace, putting on
the armour of justice, seizing the shield of salvation, and
sharpening the 'sword of the spirit which is the Word of
God'. (Eph. 6:13–17) This is how the Apostle [Paul]
prepares us for battle. Such are the arms that make us
invulnerable.[10]

Even after Constantine, the church still cried out against
violence and regarded violent people as barred from
communion. As St. John Chrysostom, Doctor of the
Church and Archbishop of Constantinople, preached late
in the fourth century:

> It is certainly a finer and a more wonderful thing to
> change the mind of enemies and to bring them to another
> way of thinking than to kill them (especially when they
> were only Twelve and the world was full of wolves). We
> ought to be ashamed of ourselves, we who act so very
> differently [than the Apostles] and rush like wolves upon
> our foes. So long as we are sheep, we have the victory;
> but if we are wolves, we are beaten — for then the help
> of the shepherd is withdrawn from us, for he feeds sheep
> not wolves . . . [And can we dare to receive communion
> if we are violent people?] What excuse shall we have if,
> eating of the Lamb [of Christ], we become as wolves?
> If, led like sheep into pasture, we behave as though we
> were ravening lions? This mystery requires that we
> should be innocent not only of violence but of all enmity,
> however slight, for this is the mystery of peace.[11]

One finds pastors in our own time with a similar understanding of the church, for example Father Elias Chacour
in Galilee. Not only among Palestinians but among many
Jews, he has become one of the most respected people of
northern Israel. Now, through his autobiography, *Blood
Brothers*, he is becoming well known in many countries.

Elias lives in Ibillin, an ancient hilltop village near Haifa
surrounded by olive trees, some of them older than Chris-

tianity. Today his congregation is thriving. They have built a regional high school, opened a community centre, and established a large library. In the library is a beautiful sign in Arabic with this text:

> God is the creator of all human beings, with their differences, their colours, their races, their religions. Be attentive: Every time you draw nearer to your neighbour, you draw nearer to God. Be attentive: Every time you go further from your neighbour, you go further from God.

When Elias was first sent to that town many years ago, there was no community centre or library and neighbours were far apart. The church was falling down and the small congregation that worshipped inside was in no better condition than the building. The divisions that ran through the parish could be seen in the way that people arranged themselves in the church on Sunday: four distinct groups each keeping a distance from the others, and everyone with grim faces. The fundamental division in the church was between four brothers; even the death of their mother had not provided the occasion for the brothers to be in the same room together.

On Palm Sunday of his first year as pastor of Ibillin, Elias looked from the front of the church at the stony faces before him. One of the brothers, a policeman, sat in the front row with his wife and children. Hymns were sung, but without any spirit. There were readings from the Bible, and then a sermon. 'The congregation endured me indifferently,' Elias recalls, 'fulfilling their holiday obligation to warm the benches.' But before the service ended, he did something no-one, perhaps not even he himself, had anticipated. He walked to the back of the church and padlocked the door.

Returning to the front of the church, he told his parishioners, 'Sitting in this building does not make you a Christian. You are a people divided. You argue and hate each other. You gossip and spread lies. Your religion is a lie. If you can't love your brother whom you see, how can you say that you love God who is invisible? You have allowed the Body of Christ to be disgraced. I have tried for months to unite you. I have failed. I am only a man. But there is someone else who can bring you together in true unity. His name is Jesus Christ. He has the power to forgive you. So now I will be quiet and allow him to give you that power. If you will not forgive, then we stay locked in here. If you want, you can kill each other, and I'll provide your funeral gratis.'

Ten minutes passed, but for Elias they seemed like hours. At last the policeman stood up, faced the congregation, bowed his head and said, 'I am sorry. I am the worst of all. I have hated my own brothers. I have hated them so much that I wanted to kill them. More than any of you, I need forgiveness.'

He turned to Elias. 'Father, can you forgive me?'

'Come here,' Elias replied. They embraced each other with the kiss of peace. 'Now go and greet your brothers.'

The four brothers rushed together, meeting halfway down the aisle, and in tears forgave each other.

'In an instant,' Elias recalls, 'the church was a chaos of embracing and repentance.'

Elias had to shout to make his next words audible. 'Dear friends, we are not going to wait until next week to celebrate the Resurrection. Let us begin it now. We were dead to each other. Now we are alive again.' He began to sing, 'Christ is risen from the dead. By his death he has trampled death and given life to those in the tomb.' The congregation joined in the hymn. Unchaining the door, Elias led them into the streets.

'For the rest of the day and far into the evening, I joined groups of believers as they went from house to house. At every door, someone had to ask forgiveness for a certain wrong. Never was forgiveness withheld.'[12]

12: A life centred on the works of mercy

It is this biblical understanding of engaged, forgiving, demanding love that the saintly Father Zosima speaks of in Dostoyevsky's novel, *The Brothers Karamazov*. Fr. Zosima, an old, Russian Orthdox monk near the end of his life, is daily sought by pilgrims. On one occasion he is confronted by a wealthy woman racked with doubt about the existence of God. She asks how she can find certainty in matters of faith.

'There's no proving it,' Fr. Zosima tells her, 'though you can be convinced of it'.

'How?'

'By the experience of active love. Strive to love your neighbour actively and tirelessly. As you advance in love you will grow surer of the reality of God and of the immortality of your soul. If you attain to perfect self-forgetfulness in the love of your neighbour, then you will believe without doubt, and no doubt can possibly enter your soul. This has been tried. This is certain.'

The woman says that she loves humanity to such an extent that sometimes she imagines abandoning everything and becoming a sister of mercy, binding up wounds, even kissing them, but then she wonders whether those she served would be grateful or whether instead they might not respond with complaints and abuse. Dreading ingratitude, she does nothing.

Fr. Zosima responds: 'Love in action is a harsh and dreadful thing compared with love in dreams. Love in dreams thirsts for immediate action, rapidly performed and in the sight of all. People will even give their lives if only the ordeal does not last long but is soon over, with all looking on and applauding as though on the stage. But active love is labour and fortitude . . .'

One of the people who centred her life in active love was Dorothy Day, founder of the Catholic Worker movement in the United States. She read Dostoyevsky's books again and again and knew the Fr. Zosima passages from *The Brother Karamazov* by heart. It was no surprise to her when she discovered that Fr. Zosima was modelled on a monk Dostoyevsky knew quite well: Fr. Amvrosy of the Hermitage of Optino in central Russia. For Dorothy Day, Fr. Zosima had always been as real as an old friend sitting at her side.

Dorothy Day was a woman who had much in common with the disciple of active love, St. Francis of Assisi: both had an attraction to the poor, which led her to live among them, and a commitment to live out the most radical teachings of Jesus, including the renunciation of violence. Like Francis, she started a movement that was meant for anyone, not only the unmarried. The movement she began in 1933 has led to the foundation of houses of hospitality in many parts of the United States. The newspaper she edited, *The Catholic Worker*, today has more than 100,000 subscribers.

The first issue of *The Catholic Worker* appeared in May, 1933, in the midst of the Great Depression. It sold, and still sells, for a penny a copy — priced to be affordable for those out of work. Dorothy's first editorial said the new paper would show its readers that the church is concerned not only with spiritual welfare but also with material welfare. The paper caught on. Within a few months there were thousands of readers.

What she had envisioned only as a newspaper quickly became a movement. First in New York, then in other cities, Catholic Worker communities were formed as places of welcome for homeless people (the houses are in the down-and-out areas like New York City's Bowery). Anyone was welcome. No questions were asked. There were no forms to fill out or sermons to endure while you ate your soup. The Catholic Worker, in common with the Holy

Rule of St. Benedict, believed that 'each person should be received as Christ'. No programmes of self-improvement were imposed on those who came through the door.

Dorothy was often criticized for her non-institutional response to those who were living ragged lives on the street. A social worker visiting the Catholic Worker house in New York asked Dorothy how long her guests were 'allowed' to stay.

'We let them stay forever,' Dorothy replied. 'They live with us, they die with us, and we give them a Christian burial. We pray for them after they are dead. Once they are taken in, they become members of the family. Or rather they always were members of the family. They are our brothers and sisters in Christ.'[13]

Dom Helder Camara, the Brazilian bishop who has a great deal in common with Dorothy Day, has said, 'When I give bread to the hungry, they call me a saint. When I ask why the hungry have no bread, they call me a Communist.' Certainly that happened to Dorothy although she never belonged to any political party. She was political only in the sense that she could not live in peace with a social order that caused so much hunger and suffering. She was political in the sense that she saw that the gospel has to do with life as a whole, not only with how *I* live but how we live together. She believed that the gospel challenges all that makes life wretched. 'Our problems,' she said plainly, 'stem from our acceptance of this filthy, rotten system.'

She was often imprisoned as a result of her activity in union, peace, and civil rights movements. One of my favourite photos of Dorothy, taken in 1973 when she was 76 years old, shows her holding the sack-like prison dress she wore the last time she was behind bars. On that occasion she was arrested in California with Mexican-American farm workers who were struggling to form a union. All the women who were arrested with her signed their names on her rough garment, making it a treasure to her.

There had been no pacifist movement in the Catholic Church for centuries, until the Catholic Worker. Perhaps more than anyone since St. Francis, Dorothy Day began a process within Catholicism that put Jesus, rather than the just-war theologians, at the centre of the church's social life.

'We see that the works of mercy oppose the works of war,' she said. 'The works of mercy call us to feed the hungry, but war creates hunger. We are required to clothe the naked, but war burns the skins from people's bodies. We are called to welcome the homeless, but war creates millions of refugees. We are called to take care of the sick, but even sickness is a weapon in war. We are called to visit the prisoner, but war makes thousands into prisoners of war. We would rather be with Our Lord in prison than killing him on a battlefield.'

Dorothy died on November 29, 1980. It was a widely marked event in America, not only noticed by Christians of every variety but by many people in other religious traditions, or outside every religion. By then many regarded her as one of Christianity's great reformers and a modern saint, though Dorothy herself had once said, 'Don't call me a saint — I don't want to be dismissed so easily'.

Dorothy Day cannot be easily dismissed. Countless people revere her memory and live more adventurous lives of faith because of the example she gave of overcoming enmity in a life of active love.

Making Friends

1: Questioning enmity in my own life

We often avoid hard, crisp words, preferring cosmetic expressions that seem to legitimize what would otherwise be illegitimate. No one, for example, advocates killing an unborn human; abortion is recommended, not killing; and the object of the abortion is designated a foetus: two Latin words mask the awful truth of homespun English. Political and military leaders speak of defence, rather than war. The horrors commited by one's own nation are described as necessary to preserve national security, while similar acts done by an opponent are condemned as terrorism.

Enemy is a little-used word. Perhaps it gives reality too sharp an edge, or perhaps it is too biblical for the post-Christian world. Only in wartime is the word widely used.

In fact many situations of enmity exist and intercept everyone's daily life: in the family, workplace, neighbourhood, nation and between nations. Hardly a single page in any daily newspaper fails to contain vivid reminders of how much enmity surrounds us and what it is costing in suffering, despair and death.

Even so, if one is to judge by the rarity of sermons on the subject, we Christians seem to think that the commandment to love our enemies has very little to do with us.

Before such a commandment can find a response in our lives, one has to take the step of admitting ways in which enmity is real in one's own life and community. Once I have confessed to myself that I have enemies, I have a starting point. Until then, the gospel can have little to do with the main events in my life.

Would you be willing to take that step? Would you be willing to clearly specify to yourself who your enemies are?

Would you be willing to write down the names of your enemies? Would you name specific persons or sorts of persons you dislike and whose company you avoid?

Think about individuals it distresses you to see: in your own family, in the neighbourhood, where you work.

Think of individuals who have hurt you or hurt those in your care.

Think about categories of people that are defined by racial, religious, sexual, economic or national labels.

Think of people who are the current or potential targets of weapons and forces that in some way you support, passively or actively, through your work or taxes or other activities.

Write down the names or group labels, even if you are still hesitant to call them enemies. Think about each name label on your list. In each case, picture faces or images. Give yourself at least a minute for each name or label.

Go back to the beginning of your list. Consider in each case how the enmity began. Consider incidents or reasons that justify your feelings. Consider ways in which it has shaped your life and activity.

Take the point of view of those you have listed. Are they actually your enemies? Or are there cases in which there are grounds for some doubt? What have you done that might justify their hostility?

Have you prayed for all those people you have listed? What sort of prayer? Has it been prayer simply to have things your own way? Or prayer that the others become the sort of person you are? Has it been prayer rooted in real caring?

Have you talked to people who might help or intervene in a constructive way?

Have you searched for points of possible agreement? Have you allowed yourself to be aware of qualities which are admirable in those you have listed?

Consider what might happen to you, to others, if this enmity continues: shattered friendship, division among co-workers, loss of employment, separation, divorce, court battles, war and, finally, the destruction of the world in nuclear war.

Try to imagine what you could do that might help bring this enmity to an end. How can you help to convert enmity to friendship?

2: The disciplines of active love

Overcoming enmity is not something we do by ourselves. We need others to help. For example, problems in a marriage often benefit from the help of a skilled and caring marriage counsellor. Similarly, conflict resolution between groups of people and states involves not only a few political leaders and specialists but large numbers of people.

In our endeavours to overcome enmity, however, help from others is often not enough. At the deepest level, we depend on God to give us the strength to love, and we need to ask God to give us that strength. We need to think about Jesus, who not only gave us the commandment to love our enemies but provides us with crucial information about how to do it, and is with us in ways we can hardly imagine.

Reflecting on the word and example of Jesus, we can identify seven disciplines of active love that are essential aspects of personal and group response to enmity:

> *Praying for enemies*
> *Doing good to enemies*
> *Turning the other cheek*
> *Offering forgiveness*
> *Breaking down the dividing wall of enmity*
> *Offering non-violent resistance to evil*
> *Recognizing Jesus in others*

The pages that follow will reflect on each of these disciplines.

3: Praying for enemies

'But I say to you,' Jesus said in the Sermon on the Mount, 'love your enemies and *pray for those who persecute you.*' (Matt. 5:44)

One of the masters of the spiritual life in our own century was a Russian monk, Staretz Simeon Silouan, an uneducated peasant who was born in 1866 and lived until 1938. He was an immensely strong man who, in his youth, had a volcanic temper. During a feast day celebrating the patron saint of his village, he was playing a concertina when two brothers, the village cobblers, began to tease him. The older of the brothers tried to snatch the concertina from Silouan and a fight broke out between them.

'At first I thought of giving in to the fellow,' Silouan told a fellow monk later in his life, 'but then I was ashamed at how the girls would laugh at me, so I gave him a great hard blow in the chest. His body shot away and he fell backwards with a heavy thud in the middle of the road. Froth and blood trickled from his mouth. All the onlookers were horrified. So was I. "I've killed him," I thought, and stood rooted to the spot . . . For a long time the cobbler lay where he was. It was over half an hour before he could rise to his feet. With difficulty they got him home, where he was bad for a couple of months, but he didn't die.'

Silouan felt ever after that there was only the slightest difference between himself and a murderer. As time passed, he found himself drawn towards life of prayer and penance.

After becoming a monk with a monastic community on Mount Athos, he thought and prayed deeply about violence and its causes. A profound sense of human inter-connectedness was one of God's gifts to him. He realized that 'through Christ's love, everyone is made an inseparable part of our own, eternal existence . . . for the Son of Man has taken within himself all mankind.'[15]

One of the US astronauts, Russell Schweickart, had a similar sense of this oneness when he looked at the earth from his window in space as he neared the moon:

[You see] the earth not as something big . . . [but] as a small thing out there. And the contrast between that bright blue and white Christmas tree ornament and the black sky, that infinite universe, really comes through, and the size of it, the significance of it. It is so small and fragile and such a precious little spot in that universe that you can block it out with your thumb, and you realize that on that small spot, that little blue and white thing, is everything that means anything to you — all of history, and music and poetry and art and death and birth and love, all the tears, joy, games, all of it on that little spot out there that you can cover with your thumb. And you realize from that perspective that you've changed, that there's something new there, that the relationship is no longer what it was.[16]

Staretz Silouan had no spaceship window and probably could not have imagined anyone flying to the moon, but the life of prayer provided the same discovery: we really are God's children, it really is one human family, and the earth is as small as a kitchen table in God's eyes. Little by little he came to the conviction that love of enemies is not simply an aspect of Christian life but is 'the central criterion of true faith and of real communion with God, the lover of souls, the lover of humankind.'

Without prayer for enemies, he realized, we are powerless to love them. In fact the only love we can offer is God's own love. Prayer can give us access to God's love for those we would otherwise regard with disinterest, irritation, fear, or active hostility.

Jesus was relating to all sorts of people who were either

hostile to him or hostile to each other, though he was never the enemy of any person. Yet we know he was subject to the same temptations we are; his 40-day fast in the desert was a time of excruciating temptation with only meditation and prayer as a shield.

His advice for practising love of enemies begins with prayer.

What is prayer? In introducing a book of photographs of people praying, the photographer Abraham Menashe comments:

> Prayer is a deeply personal act through which we commune, petition, reach out, and give thanks . . . Prayer is present in all aspects of life . . . When we attend to prayer, its nature becomes known to us. We take refuge in stillness, and in our most naked state become receptive to a life force that nourishes, heals, and makes us whole again. To the extent that we have the courage to seek moments of solitude and listen to our inner voice, we will be guided by a light that lives in us. We will come to know a love that does not disappoint — peace the world does not offer.[17]

'When we attend to prayer, its nature becomes known to us.' An early discovery each person makes is that prayer is far more than reciting words, yet the repetition of sacred texts has remained important in every religious tradition. The psalms, expressing so many aspects of life, remain a school of prayer for each generation.

Prayer — like the psalms — takes the great longings, joys, sorrows, griefs, rages and fears of our life and world into that part of ourselves which longs and reaches toward God. Prayer is the opening of one's life to God.

One of the people of prayer who has most inspired me was an old Russian woman I came to know only through the autobiography of her grandson, Maxim Gorky. As a child, he watched her praying aloud before her candle-lit icon in the corner of her room. Maxim listened with such rapt attention that, writing about her years later, his memories were still vivid and detailed.

'She always prayed for a long time after a day of quarrels and aggravation [for she was married to a violent, quarrelsome husband]. She told God about everything that had happened in the house, down to the last detail. Massive, like a mountain, she would kneel down and start off very quickly and in an unintelligible whisper, and then deepened her voice to a loud grumble.

' "As you know too well, God, everyone wants the best of things. Mikhail, the elder, should really stay in the town, and he wouldn't like it if he had to go across the river, where everything's new and hasn't been tried out yet. I've no idea what will happen. Father has more love for Yakov. Do you think it's a good thing to love one child more than the other? He's an obstinate old man. Please, God, make him see reason!"

'As she looked at the dim icon with her large, shining eyes, she instructed God, "Let him have a dream which will make him understand how to give himself to both his sons!" '

The grandmother went on and on, reflecting before God, with God, about each person in the house and then branching out into the neighbourhood. She would, at times, cross herself, bow down to the floor and even, in moments of anguish, bang her head against the floorboards. At times there were extended silences, so long that her grandson thought that perhaps she had fallen asleep, but then she recovered her voice and continued the dialogue.

After one long silence, her grandson remembered her saying, 'What else? Save all believers. Forgive me, stupid fool that I am. You know that I don't sin on purpose, but only because I'm stupid.' Then she sighed and added in a warm, contented voice, 'Dear God, you know everything that goes on.'[18]

To pray whole-heartedly becomes the most vital force in life. Not only does it empower us in countless ways, but it reaches others, including those we view as enemies, through hidden channels.

In praying for our enemies, we are not hurling holy thoughts at them or petitioning God to make them into copies of ourselves. Rather we are bringing our enemies into that part of ourselves which is deepest and most vulnerable. We are begging God for the good of those whom, at other times, we wished to harm.

In praying for enemies, we are asking God to use us for the well-being of those we fear.

At the same time, we are asking to see ourselves as we are seen by those who fear us, so that we can see enmity not only from our side but from the other side. For we not only *have* enemies; we *are* enemies.

In such prayer, even if it is prayer without words, we are appealing to God for the strength to love, appealing not only for the conversion of our adversaries but for our own conversion. We ourselves may be harder to convert than our adversaries. As Gandhi, a saint with a sense of humour, once remarked: 'I have only three enemies. My favourite enemy, the one most easily influenced for the better, is the British nation. My second enemy, the Indian people, is far more difficult. But my most formidable opponent is a man named Mohandas K. Gandhi. With him I seem to have very little influence.'

In praying for enemies, it may help to spend periods of time simply looking at a photo of that enemy, or, in the case of group enemies, to use photos that help you to connect. Newspapers and books can be a good source for photos to use in prayer. As you quietly look at the picture, you may find it helpful to recite the Jesus prayer (used almost continuously by Staretz Silouan of Mount Athos, so that it was as much a part of him as breathing): *'Lord Jesus Christ, Son of the living God, have mercy on me, a sinner.'*

4: Doing good to our enemies

Jesus calls us not only to prayer but to action: *'Do good to those who hate you, bless those who curse you.'* (Luke 6:28) Prayer is not an alternative to action; in fact prayer may empower us to take personal responsibility for what we wish others would do, or God would grant in some miraculous way without our having to lift a finger.

Contrary to popular belief, Jesus' teaching about a compassionate response to enemies was not new doctrine. We find in the Mosaic Law:

> If you meet your enemy's ox or his donkey going astray, you shall bring it back to him. If you see the donkey of one who hates you lying under a burden, you shall refrain from leaving him with it. (Exodus 23:4–5)

The Jews were forbidden to destroy the fruit trees of enemies or to poison their wells, and the Book of Proverbs actually calls for positive acts of caring for the well-being of adversaries: 'If your enemy is hungry, give him bread.' (25:21) This was taken up by St. Paul:

> Bless those who persecute you; bless and do not curse them. Rejoice with those who rejoice, weep with those who weep. Live in harmony with one another; do not be haughty, but associate with the lowly; never be conceited. Repay no one evil for evil, but take thought for what is noble in the sight of all. If possible, so far as it depends upon you, live peaceably with all. Beloved, never avenge yourselves, but leave it to the wrath of God; for it is written, 'Vengeance is mine, I will repay,

says the Lord'. No, if your enemy is hungry, feed him; if he is thirsty, give him drink; for by doing so you will reap burning coals upon his head. Do not be overcome by evil, but overcome evil with good. (Rom. 12:14–21)

Paul is simply amplifying the ordinary teaching of Jesus. He does so without encouraging unrealistic expectations that peace can be obtained simply by one's own peaceable behaviour. The suffering that Jews and Christians had experienced despite the most exemplary behaviour was clear evidence that there was sometimes no defence at all against the evil done by others. Paul must have often recalled the stoning of Stephen, whose death he had witnessed and which occurred with his consent; Paul may even have been among those actually throwing the stones. (Acts 7:58–60)

Paul calls on Christians to live peaceably with others no matter how unpeaceful those others may be, and in no case to seek revenge. If vengeance is required, he says, that is God's business. But for followers of Jesus, far from striking back at those who strike us, we are to do what is 'noble in the sight of all', responding with care to the needs of our enemies. In doing so, he says, we place 'burning coals' around the enemy's head. This is like the 'burning coal' with which God purified the mouth of the prophet Isaiah so that he could preach God's thoughts rather than his own. Good deeds done to enemies may similarly purify their thoughts and lead them in an entirely different direction.

Alfred Hassler, the former secretary of the Fellowship of Reconciliation (FOR) in the United States, tells an amazing story of something that happened in the early 1950s, just after the Korean War:

There was a famine in China, extremely grave. At the time, Communist China was shelling two islands, Quemoy and Matsu, military bases of Taiwan, a US ally. Another war seemed about to start in Asia. Many people in the US thought the thing to do was to use nuclear weapons against China, and we now know that this was what the Pentagon's Joint Chiefs of Staff were recommending to President Eisenhower.

The FOR response to all this was to launch a campaign for famine relief in China. We manufactured thousands of small cotton sacks, not even as big as a postcard, with a draw string at one end and, on the other, a mailing label addressed to the President. The message on these little sacks was. *'If thine enemy hunger, feed him. Send surplus grain to China.'* We invited people to put some grain or breakfast cereal in these sacks and mail them to the White House.

Given the fact that this campaign was going on during the McCarthy period when anyone who used the word 'peace' was likely to be called a communist, the campaign got a remarkably positive reception. A lot of churches took part, and after some time there was even a story about it on the front page of *The New York Times*. But months passed, interest dropped off and finally we gave it up. The White House 'made no comment,' as they say. No surplus food was sent to China. Many thousands died of hunger while US surplus grain was being eaten by rats. Some of the grain was stored on disused Navy ships right on the Hudson River at West Point — you could actually hear the sounds of the rats eating grain if the wind was blowing in the right direction.

Twenty years later, I happened to meet someone who had been a member of Eisenhower's staff. He recognized my name and told me that the FOR campaign, which we thought had been entirely ignored at the White House, had in fact been discussed at three separate cabinet meetings! At these same cabinet meetings there was discussion of the recommendation from the Joint Chiefs of Staff that the US attack China. At the third meeting, President Eisenhower turned to the cabinet member responsible for the Food for Peace Program and asked, 'How many of those grain bags have come in?' The answer was 45,000, plus tens of thousands of letters.

Eisenhower's response was to say to the Pentagon people that if that many Americans were trying to find a conciliatory solution with China, it wasn't time to launch a war with China. The proposal was vetoed.

Of course there was no letter to us from the President thanking us for helping him make up his mind, and there was no press conference to announce the decision not to go to war. For many years we thought what we had done had been a complete failure. It was just a chance encounter that revealed to us that, while we had failed in one way, we had helped accomplish something else that saved millions of lives.[19]

The teaching to do good to enemies is viewed as particularly idealistic and profoundly unrealistic. In fact, it is a teaching full of common sense. Unless we want to pave the way to a tragic future, we must search for opportunities through which we can demonstrate to an opponent our longing for an entirely different kind of relationship. An adversary's moment of need or crisis can provide that opening.

This is precisely what the Samaritan was doing to the Jew he found dying on the side of the road in Jesus' parable of the compassionate enemy (Luke 20:30–37). In offering help to an enemy in his distress, he immediately altered or even destroyed the wounded Jew's stereotype of Samaritans, the enemy image he held. That man would never again think of Samaritans without gratitude.

The very last thing our enemies imagine is that we could wish them well or do them well.

But care must be taken that our constructive responses are not simply public relations gestures. Even if our gestures are quite sincere, there is still the possibility they will be seen as insincere. Notice that every disarmament initiative taken by the Soviet Union is invariably dismissed as 'just propaganda'.

In fact the motives behind any action humans take — not only the motives of heads of state — can be extraordinarily complex. I often think about a letter of caution that Thomas Merton wrote to friends in the peace movement during the Vietnam war:

> [We must] always direct our action toward opening people's eyes to the truth, and if they are blinded, we must try to be sure we did nothing specifically to blind them. Yet there is that danger: the danger one observes subtly in tight groups like families and monastic communities [and groups seeking social change], where the martyr for the right sometimes thrives on making his persecutors terribly and visibly wrong. He can drive them in desperation to be wrong, to seek refuge in the wrong, to seek refuge in violence.[20]

Often gesture must follow gesture. It is the second mile Jesus asked us to walk. The most insignificant gesture may prove to be the most transforming.

5: Turning the other cheek

In the Sermon on the Mount, Jesus says,

> If someone strikes you on the cheek, offer him the other also. (Matt. 5:39; Luke 6:23)

How different this is from the advice provided in the average film or novel! There the constant message is: If you are hit, hit back. Let your blow be harder than the one you received. In fact, you need not be hit at all in order to strike others. Provocation, irritation, or the expectation of attack is warrant enough.

I remember someone in my unit in the Navy who borrowed a dollar from me and then never got around to giving it back. He had the job of distributing the mail every day, a job with an ounce of power among lonely people starved for letters from home. Wearing the role as if it were a crown, he was not above delaying delivery of a letter addressed to anyone who annoyed him, and little by little we all came to regard him with loathing.

One morning I demanded the return of my dollar. He looked at me with contempt, reached into his pocket, took out a dollar bill, held it in front of my face and then dropped it on the floor.

Leaving the money where it was, I grabbed him under the arms, lifted him off the floor and threw him against the wall. It still amazes me to remember how light he felt, how easily I made his body fly across the room. He came back with his fists flying. Far from being alarmed, I rejoiced in the combat, hammered away, hardly aware of the crowd that gathered around us. The fight might well have gone

on until I had done him some real harm, had not the bell
summoned us to inspection. As we stood at attention
outside the barracks, I remember taking great pride in
his bloodied lip and bruised face. Fortunately, when the
inspecting officer asked him what had happened to his face,
he told the prescribed lie — he had tripped on the stairs.

This battle won me a good deal of admiration at the time.
I was immensely pleased with myself. The fight remains a
shiny memory, though I was astonished (and alarmed) to
discover what strength and deadly will I possessed when
my anger was sufficiently aroused. Quite possibly that fight
had something to do with the particular attention I later
gave, when my conversion to Christianity began, to what
the New Testament has to say about violence, for by then
I knew this was not something directed at other people.
(Less than two years after my conversion began, having
become a conscientious objector, I was granted an early
discharge.)

'Turning the other cheek' is often seen as an especially
suspect Christian doctrine. Some see it as promoting an
ethic of self-abasement that borders on masochism (the
psychosis of deriving pleasure from mistreatment). Others
would say it is Jesus at his most unrealistic: 'Human beings
just aren't made that way.' For a great many people the
problem can be put even more simply: 'Turning the other
cheek isn't manly.' In fact it is quite manly, quite human,
and very sensible.

One of the manliest men I know, Jean Goss, was a
partisan in the French resistance during World War II, a
brave, but also quite deadly man, whose conversion to
Christianity and a non-violent way of life occurred while
he was a prisoner of the Nazis. Jean sometimes tells a story
from his days as a prisoner during the war:

> When Jesus was being beaten by the Roman soldiers, he
> wasn't silent. He said to his torturers: 'Why do you strike
> me?' If Jesus had been like me, he would have kept
> quiet, because if you speak, you run the risk of another

blow, or worse. All the same, it's strange. There was no second slap. Only the strongest are capable of turning the other cheek. It stops the massacre. It goes even further: it doesn't allow the other fellow to call himself a brute. I remember one of our guards in Germany. He had come back from the Russian front and sometimes had fits of raving madness. He would get carried away and start beating prisoners. One of them had the courage to go up to him and say, 'I'm volunteering. If you need to brutalize someone, hit me.' The torturer couldn't believe his ears. 'How many blows do you want?' 'I leave that to your conscience,' answered the prisoner. That was the last straw, the thing you couldn't say: conscience. 'I'm a brute, an instrument, I'm not a conscience. I have no conscience. I haven't got the right to have a conscience.' It took him some time to realize the opposite, that he had a conscience, but the flogging stopped.[21]

Something similar happened to Jean's wife, Hildegard. In 1975, she and Adolfo Perez Esquivel (Adolfo received the Nobel Peace Prize in 1980) were arrested in Brazil. In prison, the guards blindfolded them and made them listen to amplified recordings of prisoners being tortured. This went on for two days until the Archbishop of Sao Paulo, Cardinal Arns, was able to convince the military authorities to let them go. The guards were ordered to feed them first, but Hildegard and Adolfo refused food. They said they wanted to fast because they acknowledged that they themselves, just like their guards, were responsible for the injustice in the world. They wanted to fast to free themselves from all the resentment towards these same guards and allow their consciences to open up.

Often a person is hit because he is in the way. It is punishment for being there, and a warning to move on immediately or worse will be done to you. To turn the other cheek is not to give in and get out of the way; even at the risk of receiving another blow, you stay where you are but at the same time you refuse to respond with violence.

There is always risk in standing in the way of violent people. But there are times when one's faith and conscience lead one to risk even life itself. Consider one incident of collective 'cheek turning' by devout Jews in Judaea in 26 AD, just a few years before Jesus' execution. Flavius Josephus writes this account:

> The Jews rose up against Pilate in Caesarea to ask him to take the statues [of the emperor, regarded by the Jews as idols] away from Jerusalem . . . When Pilate refused, they encamped around his house for five days and five nights. On the sixth day Pilate went before his tribunal in the great stadium and called the Jews together under the pretext of wanting to respond to their wishes. Then he gave armed soldiers the command to encircle the Jews. When the Jews saw how they were surrounded . . . they remained silent. Pilate, after declaring that he would have them killed it they would not honour the image of the emperor, gave the soldiers the sign to draw their swords. But the Jews threw themselves on the ground as if at a single command and offered their necks, all prepared to die rather than to violate God's law. Overcome by their religious zeal, Pilate gave the command to have the statues removed from Jerusalem.[22]

But we need not look back across twenty centuries for examples of brave men and women standing their ground, risking not only injury but their lives in order to 'be obedient to God rather than man'. (Acts 5:29) There are countless examples in our own century.

Remember the many thousands of American Christians who joined Martin Luther King in standing peacefully in the way of those who were intent on maintaining racist divisions. They received many blows, stood ready to receive more, but never struck back. Some died, many were injured, thousands were imprisoned, but from their brave struggle Americans (and many others) began to repent of racism and Christians developed a more profound understanding of discipleship.

Rosa Parks is one of the less known figures in the movement associated with Martin Luther King, but had it not been for her, perhaps his name would still be unknown. She was active in a local black church and had been the local secretary of the National Association for the Advancement of Coloured People. In 1955, when King (fresh out of divinity school) was a newly appointed pastor in Montgomery, Alabama, Rosa Parks was working as a seamstress in a Montgomery department store.

On December 1, at the end of her working day and after doing her shopping, she boarded a public bus:

'When I got on the bus, I noticed the bus driver [was the man who had once] evicted me from the bus because I had refused to pay my fare in the front and then get out and go around to the back to get in. Sometimes you would pay your fare, get out, start walking to the back of the bus, and then it would pull away before you got back in. They just left you behind!

'By the time I got on, the Negro section in the back of the bus was filled. But there was one vacant seat in the middle section the part we could use as long as no white people wanted the seats . . .

'On the third stop a few white people boarded the bus and they took all the designated white seats. There was one white man left standing. The driver turned around and said he needed those front seats so this white man could take a seat, which meant the ones we [four black people] were sitting in. The four of us would have to stand up in order to accommodate this one white passenger. This was segregation.

'When the driver first spoke, none of us moved. But then he spoke a second time with what I call a threat. He said, "You all better make it light on yourselves and let me have those seats." At that point the other three stood up . . .

'The driver looked at me and asked me if I was going to stand up. I told him no, I wasn't. He said, "If you don't stand up, I'm going to have you arrested." I told him to go on and have me arrested. I was too tired to stand. I didn't exchange any more words with him.'

Rosa Parks was arrested, taken to the police station, her things taken away, and she was locked in a cell. She requested a drink of water but it was denied; the drinking fountain was for whites only. 'I wasn't happy at all,' she remembers, 'but I don't recall being extremely frightened. I just felt very much annoyed and inconvenienced because I had hoped to go home and cook supper and do whatever I had to do for the evening. But now I was sitting in jail and couldn't get home.'[23]

That night a black lawyer, E. D. Nixon, bailed her out and promised he would defend her in court. Nixon phoned the ministers of the black churches in Montgomery and told them what had happened to Rosa Parks. That same night 40 pastors, among them the young Martin Luther King, met together and decided the time was right to try to end segregation on Montgomery's public transportation system. They agreed to begin a black boycott of the buses. Martin Luther King was elected to head the boycott, partly because, being the youngest, he had the least to lose should the campaign fail.

Several days after Rosa Park's arrest, a city judge found her guilty and ordered her to pay a $14 fine plus court costs. A year later, the US Supreme Court, deciding that racial segregation in public transportation violated the US Constitution, overturned her conviction. It was a major blow to the legal foundations of segregation everywhere in the United States. But the birth of the Civil Rights Movement came not from a court ruling; it came from the actions of ordinary people in a small southern city. The blacks of Montgomery had walked many thousands of miles without boarding a bus, had endured threats, abuse and violence. Many had been jailed, and the home of the King family had been bombed.

December 21, 1956, was an historic day. Martin Luther King (sitting next to a white pastor, Glenn Smiley of the Fellowship of Reconciliation Staff) and Rosa Parks rode together on Alabama's first integrated public bus.

'We will match your capacity to inflict suffering,' Dr. King had said, 'with our capacity to endure suffering. We will meet your physical force with soul force. We will not hate you, but we cannot in good conscience obey your injust laws . . . and in winning our freedom, we will win you in the process.'

6: Forgiveness

One of the saints of the early church, Abbot Moses, had a witty way of living the gospel. He was once asked to take part in a community meeting which was preparing to condemn a certain lax brother. The old man arrived at the meeting carrying a basket from which sand was pouring through many openings. 'Why are you doing that?' he was asked. 'You ask me to judge a brother while my own sins spill out behind me like the sand from this basket.' The embarrassed community was moved to forgive their brother.[24]

Forgiveness is at the heart of faithful living. Nothing is more fundamental to Jesus' teaching than his call to forgiveness: giving up debts, letting go of grievances, pardoning those who have harmed us. Every time we say the Lord's Prayer, we are telling God that we ask to be forgiven only in so far as we ourselves have extended forgiveness to others:

And forgive us our debts, as we also have forgiven our debtors. (Matt. 6:12; Luke 11:2–4)

A few verses later in Matthew, Jesus' teaching on this point continues:

Judge not, that you be not judged. For with the judgement you pronounce you will be judged, and the measure you give will be the measure you get. Why do you see the speck that is in your brother's eye, but do not notice the log that is in your own? (Matt. 7:1–3)

On another occasion, Peter asks Jesus how often he must extend forgiveness. 'As many as seven times?' Jesus responds,

I do not say to you seven times, but seventy times seven, (Matt. 18:22)

Jesus goes on to tell the parable of the servant whose king forgave him a huge debt, but who afterwards refused to forgive the slight debt due to him from a colleague. The king says to the unforgiving servant:

'You wicked servant! I forgave you all that debt because you besought me. Should you not have mercy on your fellow servant as I had mercy on you?' (Matt. 18:32,33)

It is not hard to identify with the servant. Who doesn't know how much easier it is to ask God to forgive us than to extend forgiveness to others? For we are wounded and the wounds often last a lifetime; they even spill across generations. As children, as parents, as husbands or wives, as families, as workers, as jobless people, as church members, as members of certain classes or races, as voters, as citizens of particular states, we have been violated, made a target, lied to, used, abandoned. Sins, often quite serious sins, have been committed against us. We may feel damaged, scarred for life, stunted. Others we love may even have died of evil done to them.

But we are not only victims. In various ways we are linked to injuries others have suffered and are suffering. If I allow myself to see how far the ripples extend from my small life, I will discover that not only in my own home but on the far side of the planet there are people who are my victims. Through what I have done or failed to do, through what my community has done or failed to do, there are others whose lives are more wretched than they might have been; there are those dying while we feast.

All the while we renew our collective preparations for a

festival of death such as the world has never before witnessed: a war fought with weapons of total annihilation. The argument is put forward that such war preparations will actually prevent the dreaded event. But, in fact, we are like children playing with matches in a sand-pit filled with gun powder.

We are moved to condemn the evils we see in others and to excuse the evils that we practise ourselves. We fail to realize that those who threaten us feel threatened by us, and often have good reasons for their fears. The problem is not simply a personal issue, for the greatest sins of enmity are committed *en masse* with very few people feeling any personal responsibility for the destruction they share in doing or preparing. 'I was only following orders' is one of humanity's most frequently repeated justifications for murder, heard as often from those who profess religious convictions as from those who deny them.

My colleague Hildegard Goss-Mayr tells a remarkable story of forgiveness that occurred in Poland ten years after the end of World War II. By then the division of Europe had become iron-hard and the arms race was underway. In Warsaw to take part in a conference, she and her husband, Jean Goss, met privately with a group of Poles to discuss the Stalinist regime that been imposed on the country and the possibilities for giving non-violent witness together whenever human rights were violated:

Defying a law prohibiting group meetings, we met in a flat with some twenty young intellectuals, all committed Christians. It was their first opportunity to meet Christians from the West. The exchange was profound and sincere. It was already late when Jean and I decided to ask a question that we knew was very much on the minds of many young West Germans we knew through the International Fellowship of Reconciliation. 'Would you be willing,' we asked, 'if the possibility should arise, to meet with Christians from West Germany? They want to ask forgiveness for what Germany did to Poland during the war and to begin to build a new relationship.' There was a silence. Finally one of our Polish friends, a young writer, jumped up and vehemently said,'Jean and Hildegard, we love you, you are our friends but what you are asking is impossible! Each stone of Warsaw has been soaked in Polish blood. We cannot forgive!'

We tried to insist: 'Who should make the first step? The non-believers? The Communists? Someone else? Or we who are baptized in the name of the One who pardoned the sin of all humanity and overcame hatred through the gift of his life?'

But our Polish friend said this was impossible. 'This is not yet the time for forgiveness.'

Even after a decade, the war wounds remained fresh and deep. Jean and I saw we could go no further. It was getting late. Before separating, we proposed that we recite together the prayer that unites us all, the Our Father. All joined in willingly. But when we got to the passage, 'and forgive us our sins as we forgive . . .', our Polish friends halted in the prayer.

Into this silence the one who had said, 'it is impossible,' spoke up in a low voice: 'I must say *yes* to you. I could no more pray the Our Father, I could no longer call myself a Christian, if I refuse to forgive. Humanly speaking, I cannot do it, but God will give us his strength!'

It was at that point that all of us understood that peace-making is impossible without conversion of the heart.

We continued to talk and plan. A year-and-a-half later, after more moderate leaders had replaced the Stalinists, ten of our Polish friends who had been in that room were given visas that allowed them to take part in a meeting in Vienna, IFOR'S first East-West conference after the war, and here they met with the Germans. From this meeting, many initiatives in East-West relations began. The friendships continue until today.[25]

Yes, I am sometimes reminded, forgiveness is a wonderful thing. But what about anger? Haven't I a right to my anger? When I am hurt, should I pretend not to feel the hurt? And if I manage to pretend, to hide my hurt and anger, am I not lying?

In fact, we can see moments of stunning anger in Jesus' life. He was furious with those who made a house of worship into a place of thieves; he was furious with those who laid heavy burdens on others which they did not carry themselves. If you want to see Jesus angry, read the 23rd chapter of Matthew's Gospel. Jesus was a passionate man and never hid his passion.

A forgiveness that is pretence, that seeks to hide pain and rage behind pretty wallpaper, is of no value. Sooner or later we will discover that the complaints are still there, still fresh, perhaps more explosive than ever. Until we allow ourselves to feel the hurt and to express it, it is unlikely an act of forgiveness will be genuine. If the forgiveness we seek to offer to those who need our forgiveness is to be of any use to them, they need to be aware of what they have done and the pain or hurt it has caused. How can they know it if we are silent? Jesus teaches that we have the obligation to speak out:

Take heed to yourselves; if your brother sins, rebuke him, and if he repents, forgive him. (Luke 17:3)

Anger has its place.

But until we have allowed ourselves to get beyond anger, to forgive, or rather to let God's forgiveness flow through us, we are burdened with our injuries and complaints every bit as much as the ghost of Jacob Marley was burdened by chains and money-boxes in Charles Dickens' *Christmas Carol.*

We are called to forgive. We need to seek forgiveness, offer forgiveness and accept forgiveness. We are followers of Jesus who taught us forgiveness even when his hands were nailed to the wood of the cross: 'Father, forgive them. They know not what they do.'

7: Breaking down the dividing wall of enmity

In Christ enmity is destroyed, Paul wrote to the church in Ephesus:

> For he is our peace, who has made us both one, and has broken down the dividing wall of enmity . . . that he might create in himself one new person in place of two, so making peace, and might reconcile us both to God in one body through the cross, thereby bringing enmity to an end. (Eph. 2:14–16)

Walls would have been on Paul's mind at the time; in the same letter he mentions that he is 'a prisoner for the Lord'. His guidance was sent from prison.

'The dividing wall of enmity' stood massively between Jews and Romans. But one day an officer of the Roman army turned to Jesus for help:

> . . . the centurion had a slave who was dear to him, who was sick and at the point of death. When he heard of Jesus, he sent to him elders of the Jews, asking him to come and heal his slave. And when they came to Jesus, they besought him earnestly, saying, 'He is worthy to have you do this for him, for he loves our nation, and he built us our synagogue.' And Jesus went with them. When he was not far from the house, the centurion sent friends to him, saying, 'Lord, do not trouble yourself, for I am not worthy to have you come under my roof . . . But say the word and let my servant be healed' . . . When Jesus heard this he marvelled at him . . . And

when those who have been sent returned to the house, they found the slave well. (Luke 7:1–10)

It must have been hard for the more zealot-minded disciples to see Jesus responding positively to the request of a Roman soldier, and galling to hear him commenting afterwards, 'I tell you, not even in Israel have I found such faith'.

Matthew comments that Jesus 'marvelled'. He marvelled at the faith of the centurion, who believed Jesus did not have to be physically present to heal. He must have been equally astonished that a soldier in a pagan army would approach a Jew with respect, and with a request rather than a command. The centurion, in fact, points out that he is used to governing others: 'I say to one, "Go," and he goes'. He had the legal right to give orders; this applied even to Roman soldiers of much lower rank. They could demand that anyone they met on the road carry their equipment for up to one Roman mile; one of them was to conscript Simon of Cyrene to carry the cross when Jesus no longer had the strength to do so. (Jesus was referring to this Roman law when he said that the faithful should then volunteer to go a *second* mile freely. (Matt. 5:41))

Jesus had a third reason to marvel; the centurion was seeking nothing for himself or a family member but rather trying to save the life of his slave. Probably the slave was Jewish. We are told that the centurion was a man who respected the Jews. Assuming that Jesus would not believe this, he sent Jewish elders to tell Jesus that this Roman loved the Jewish nation and had even contributed the money to build a synagogue.

It is an amazing story: Roman and Jew reaching out to each other, an armed man towards an unarmed man. They are brought together by a dying slave. In their encounter, the dividing wall of enmity collapses.

We live in a world of walls. Competition, contempt, repression, racism, nationalism, violence and domination: all these are seen as normal and sane. Enmity is common.

Self and self-interest, both quite narrowly defined, form the centring point in many lives. Love and the refusal to centre one's own life in enmity are dismissed as naive, idealistic, even unpatriotic, especially if one reaches out constructively to hated minorities or national enemies.

For those of us living in countries of the NATO alliance, our national enemies in recent years have been the Russians. We live in dread of their weapons, and they of ours. We are quite prepared to do much worse to them (and they to us) than take an eye for an eye. The cost is phenomenal, not only financially but in terms of millions of people busy every day in war planning and manufacture. There is the cost of suffering and death because we do so little to improve, or even maintain, the world while an arms race is going on.

There are also less tangible costs — spiritual, and psychological — for we are making the preparations for the end of the world a major part of our lives. We hear of many people who *expect* to die in a nuclear war and who live in a constant state of 'low grade' depression. Despair is widespread.

Citizens of NATO and Warsaw Pact countries are prepared to fight a nuclear war. There are even Christians who see such a war as God's will, the fulfilment of prophecies, the means whereby God will exercise judgement and cut the thread of history. They preach nuclear holocaust with enthusiasm and look forward to the ungodly being consumed while the 'elect' are lifted rapturously into heaven. Their theology could be summed up: 'And God so loved the world that he sent World War III.'

Whoever we are, whatever our views, we are, through national structures if not personal conviction, participants in major structures of enmity.

Confronted with such hostility, how can anyone hope to break through the dividing wall of enmity? How can one contribute to reconciliation?

One of the insights Thomas Merton came to in his last years was the realization that reconciliation is not simply a formal coming together of people who have been divided. It is prefigured in our spiritual lives. He wrote in his journal:

> If I can unite *in myself* the thought and devotion of Eastern and Western Christendom, the Greek and the Latin Fathers, the Russians and the Spanish mystics, I can prepare in myself the reunion of divided Christians. From that secret and unspoken unity in myself can eventually come a visible and manifest unity of all Christians. If we want to bring together what is divided, we cannot do so by imposing one division upon the other. If we do this, the union is not Christian. It is political and doomed to further conflict. We must contain all the divided worlds in ourselves and transcend them in Christ.[26]

To 'contain the divided worlds in ourselves' means that, no matter what objections we have to the Soviet political system, we have to cherish the people of the Soviet Union. And yet, far from doing so, we don't even know them. Very few in the west speak Russian; it is said that there are more *teachers* of English in the USSR than there are *students* of Russian in the United States and Britain combined.

Little objective information is offered in either public education or by the mass media about adversaries. On the contrary, in school, in the press and on television (both in news and entertainment) we are provided with images and information that can only renew our fears and preserve enmity. Through films, comic books, novels and news reports we are given vivid daily reminders of why enmity is essential.

News reports are often the hardest to guard against, for in the west we tend to view the press as an independent and objective channel of communication. But the few newspapers that actually attempt objectivity inevitably reflect national points of views. In fact few channels of mass communication even attempt global impartiality. Enemy images are forged and re-forged, images that give us no glimpse of what is human or decent in our adversaries, images that in the end condemn us to war.

In many ways the news media can be compared to a trash-collection agency. The western press collects stories about what is wrong in Russia — the Russian press collects stories of what isn't working in the west. We know a great deal about their dissidents and the shortage of consumer goods; they know about our dissidents and the unemployed. The information provided by the mass media in both alliances is mainly true, but radically incomplete. Whatever would animate sympathy, understanding or a sense of identification is generally excluded or given slight attention.

At a meeting in Assisi a few years ago, a priest of the Russian Orthodox Church said to me, 'There are not two Superpowers in the world. There are three — the USA, the USSR, and the mass media. The most dangerous is the mass media.'

To overcome the propaganda of enmity, we need to discover what Merton called 'the human dimension':

> The basic problem is not political, it is human. One of the most important things to do is to keep cutting deliberately through political lines and barriers and emphasizing that these are largely fabrications and that there is a genuine reality, totally opposed to the fictions of politics: the human dimension which politics pretends to arrogate entirely to themselves.[27]

How does one enter the human dimension of a people living far away, speaking a language we do not speak, whose lives and culture are revealed to us (more accurately, hidden from us) by a hostile mass media?

One way is to visit the Soviet Union.

My own first trip to Russia for a small meeting hosted by the Russian Orthodox Church was the occasion for my discovery of how much cold-war imagery had found its home in my own head. I became aware of this even before I stepped on the aircraft. Although flying to Moscow is no more (or less) remarkable than flying to Rome or Jerusalem, it seemed that I was on my way to another planet. I had stepped into the world of James Bond.

Once inside my hotel room, I imagined a KGB agent in some other room in the hotel listening to my rustling noises as I unpacked my suitcase. And perhaps the room *was* bugged. Secret police in every country do this kind of thing all the time. I remember that in the early 1970s we found a micro-radio concealed in the office telephone of the Emmaus House in New York City. Our community involvement in the anti-war movement meant that we were visited repeatedly by the FBI, and during one period were under daily FBI surveillance.

But there were situations in Moscow where it was possible to see that the shaping of my expectations by the cold war had little connection with reality. I love walking and even that first night decided to go for a walk. An English colleague and I walked down the wide avenue that led to Red Square, several miles to the east. It was late and the weather was wet. There were few cars and still fewer pedestrians. Even so I kept glancing around, expecting to find someone following us (another experience I had in the US during the Vietnam war). 'Surely two westerners, dissidents in the west who have links with dissidents in the east, won't be permitted to wander about unwatched.' Two hours later, past midnight, still wandering the streets of Moscow, we found ourselves totally alone. It was the first of many experiences of late-night solitude in Moscow.

Within a few days I felt quite free to wander, even to get lost, whether above ground or on the Metro beneath the streets, as I kept discovering that sooner or later I would find people who would manage to understand me and who would help me find my way.

I especially enjoyed the Moscow Metro, the underground train system. The stations really are cathedral-like. One was as baroque as a concert-hall in Mozart's day. But more interesting than the stations were the passengers. Some were soldiers in uniform, but most were wearing clothing that wouldn't stand out in either London or New York. Many were children. One child stared at me (I have a beard, which is unusual in Russia) with open curiosity. She sat on her father's lap, gripping his hand in the same way my three-year-old Anne grips mine. Her head was pressed against her father's chest.

And there were couples. Somehow I was surprised that Russians should be madly in love with each other. In a particularly crowded car during rush hour, I happened to be jammed against one pair whose heads were inclined towards each other so that their noses occasionally touched. They were oblivious of bearded Americans and everyone else in the train.

I was lucky enough to get lost over and over again and to have to turn to strangers for help. The Russians are fascinated by foreigners and are, contrary to everything I had been told, very approachable people. Anyone who hangs around a park, public square or subway platform sooner or later will be meeting Russians (maybe offering roubles for western currency or wanting to buy running shoes, but the subjects can be much more interesting).

Two students helped me from one subway platform to another, eager to practise their English. They asked me if I liked the poetry of Robert Burns. Exaggerating a bit, I said I did. They recited some of his verses and before parting we sang, 'Should auld acquaintance be forgot'. It was a rousing performance. No one on the train platform seemed to mind.

It was in the course of those walks and subway rides that I began to think afresh about Jesus' sayings on loving our enemies. This book had its beginning on the Moscow Metro.

But the most moving experiences I have had in Russia have been within churches. Few, if any, churches in the west offer the worship experience available in any Moscow church. Believers are packed together like matchsticks.

There are no chairs or pews; Russians pray standing up, with just enough room for the half bows that the Russian liturgy requires. One finds a warm welcome and many surprises, not least being the many young people in the congregation.

A Protestant friend from Sweden who had never before bowed or made the sign of the cross was scolded into doing so by the old Russian woman at her side who would not tolerate such passivity in worship. Like many western visitors, my friend was surprised how many of the people in church were *not* old women, but it is the old women who make sure no one is just standing around watching, and it was mainly these fortress-like ladies who carried the faith intact through the Stalin years.

The sung prayer in Russian churches is passionate, beautiful, and has an almost tangible quality. One Sunday while taking part in the liturgy at Moscow's Epiphany Cathedral, I felt that if the walls and pillars were taken away, the roof would stay where it was for as long as the congregation kept singing. (Unfortunately, visitors often have to strike out on their own to attend the living churches. The normal guided tours include only the museum churches like those unspeakably beautiful cathedrals within the Kremlin walls in Moscow. No doubt such churches are still places of silent prayer for many visiting Russian tourists, and have inspired many to find living churches.)

Experiences of worship in Russia have renewed and reshaped worship life within our family. At bedtime, before several Russian icons, Nancy and I now pray standing up and often we use prayers from the Orthodox liturgy.

As important and as eye-opening as travel in the Soviet Union can be, there are many things one can do to break down enmity and enter into the human dimension without ever boarding an aircraft or crossing a border.

One way to leap the world's walls without leaving home is to buy a shortwave radio and start following the news, not only from the perspective of one's own country but from the view of other countries as well. Nearly every national station does much of its broadcasting in English; Radio Moscow seems to broadcast in English from early morning until late at night. Much of it is rather two-dimensional and propagandistic, but there are occasional surprises; a recent discussion programme, for example, touched on the 'spiritual vacuum' in the USSR. Musically, you are as likely to hear Schubert's 'Ave Maria' as a communist anthem.

Better yet, there is the wonderful door of literature. The Russians are as close to you as the library and book shop: from the pre-revolutionary years, there are Pushkin, Dostoyevsky, Tolstoy, Chekov, Gogol; among the post-revolutionary authors, there are Gorki, Sholokhov, Pasternak, Soloukhin, and Yevtushenko. Though films from the USSR are rarely shown in theatres and almost never on television, occasionally they can be found in video libraries. Some offer surprisingly candid and moving views of life in the Soviet Union; one film actually won the Oscar as Best Foreign Film a few years ago, *Moscow Distrusts Tears*.

One of the most enjoyable ways to break through the wall of enmity is by sharing the table of those we are armed against. In our home, Nancy sometimes cooks 'meals of reconciliation,' serving Moscow borscht as the main dish and American apple pie for dessert.

Prayer, especially when it centres on particular people, quickly opens the human dimension. In praying for Russians, I have learned to cut out newspaper and magazine photos that catch my eye and keep them in a Bible, hymnal or prayer book. Though press photos are mainly limited to politicians, military leaders and dissidents, sometimes 'ordinary' people get into print: children, couples, old men and women. One does not need to know their names.

Taking such steps, the dividing wall of enmity breaks down. Love of enemies not only becomes possible; it becomes difficult *not* to love them. In the case of the Russians, they cease to be ideological objects but rather people enriching one's life. Even when you discover in a personal way various things you disagree with or find appalling about Soviet structures, you can no longer speak of the *people* who live in the USSR as enemies, and it is people rather than systems that are the victims of war. Structures and ideologies seem to survive wars quite well, though sometimes taking on new labels.

Beginning to know personally those who are the targets of war, praying for them daily, bringing their food to the table — these are truly disarming experiences. It becomes unthinkable to do anything which might result in their being burned alive, for truly they are our sisters and brothers. We discover that their lives are in our care, and ours in theirs.

8: Love as resistance to both evil and violence

In the Sermon on the Mount, Jesus teaches

> You have heard that it was said, 'An eye for an eye and a tooth for a tooth'. But I say to you, do not resist the one who is evil. (Matt. 5:38,39)

Jesus was a healer. He injured no one. When Peter used violence to defend Jesus, he was instantly admonished.

> Put away your sword, for whoever lives by the sword will perish by the sword. (Matt. 26:52)

Jesus' last healing miracle before the resurrection was done to an enemy, the victim of Peter's sword, a slave of the high priest who was among those who came to arrest Jesus in the Garden of Gethsemane. Jesus admonished his disciples, 'No more of this!' Then he touched the wounded man's ear and it was healed.

For several hundred years following the resurrection, the followers of Jesus were renowned (or infamous) for their refusal to perform military service. But since Constantine's Edict of Milan in 313, when church and state were first linked, Christians have been as likely as any other people to take up the sword, though there was a period in the 13th century when many Christians refused to take part in war and were given the support of church leaders for their pacifist stand. The movement St. Francis of Assisi founded for lay people, his Third Order, which many thousands joined, called on members to be peacemakers:

They are to be reconciled with their neighbours and [are] to restore what belongs to others . . . They are not to take up deadly weapons, or bear them about, against anybody . . . They are to refrain from formal oaths [which might bind them to military service] . . . They are to perform the acts of mercy: visiting and caring for the sick, burying the dead, and caring for the poor . . . They should seek the reconciliation of enemies, both among their members and among non-members.

The refusal to take up arms against enemies has always been remarkable, even scandalous, from the point of view of those in government as well as many others who see no practical alternative to armed defence. Conscientious objection has cost many years of imprisonment and suffering, even in the present century. Many have given their lives rather than perform military service, among them people recognized as saints in the early church. The issue is still a matter of debate even among Christians, though now nearly every church upholds the right of conscientious objection and many countries provide for the possibility of doing non-military alternative service.

Although increasingly Christians are living disarmed lives, it does not mean that the sword doesn't cut into their lives:

Do not think that I have come to bring peace on earth; I have come not to bring peace, but a sword. For I have come to set a man against his father, and a daughter against her mother, and a daughter-in-law against her mother-in-law; and a man's foes will be those of his own household. (Matt. 10:34–36)

In this teaching, Jesus is not authorizing hatred, only saying that the way of life he proposes will be a cause of sharp division that may even cut into family relationships. To be obedient is not always to be understood or appreciated even by those closest to you. It may lead to rejection and condemnation by those you dearly love. One has to take the risk, while doing everything possible to communicate love and respect for those who do not agree or cannot understand. Many Christians in refusing to do military service have been disowned by one or both parents. More often, family life and friendships hold together but are made more brittle.

Franz Jägerstätter, one of the conscientious objectors to emerge under Hitler's Third Reich, was fortunate that his marriage, if not all his friendships, bore the weight of the stand his conscience led him to take. His is a life worth thinking about.

An Austrian farmer living in a hamlet (St. Radegund) too small to warrant its own post office, Franz seemed, from a distance, a most ordinary man with an ordinary life. He held no academic degrees, was married and the father of three children.

He had not got off to a pious start. As a youth he was a local 'gang' leader and had been fined once for being involved in a fist fight with a gang from a neighbouring village. He had been the proud owner of a loud motorcycle. It is said that he fathered an illegitimate child (and, in fact, was himself illegitimate). None the less, his spirit was such that neighbours still regarded him as a *liaba mensch* — a 'wonderful guy'.

When, in his early 20s, Franz enrolled in voluntary religious classes conducted by the pastor of St. Radegund, his friends and neighbours must have been astonished. Perhaps it was less surprising that he was willing to raise embarrassing questions — asking, for example, if biblical texts did not suggest that Mary had other children besides Jesus.

When Franz was 29 he underwent a change described by those close to him as 'sudden and total'. One neighbour commented, 'It was almost as if he had been possessed by a higher power. It was so sudden that people just couldn't understand it.' Franz began making regular pilgrimages to a nearby shrine and never passed a church without going in to pray. He was sometimes noticed interrupting his labour in the fields to pray. For a time he thought about joining a religious community, but ultimately decided in favour of family life and farming. With his religious awakening came a deepened social concern. In 1938, when Austrians voted in favour of the national annexation with Nazi Germany, Franz resisted pressure from the pastor, mayor and many neighbours and cast the village's only dissenting vote. Whenever anyone said 'Heil Hitler', Franz responded, 'Pfui Hitler!' His stand became the subject of fierce argument in the village tavern.

It was in the summer of 1938 that he had a remarkable dream:

'I saw a beautiful shining railroad train that circled around a mountain. Streams of children — and adults as well — rushed toward the train and could not be held back.'

In his dream Franz heard a voice say that the train was going to hell. Franz was as attentive to dreams as the two Josephs of the Bible, and he thought long about the shining train. It became clear to him that the train was Nazism. He realized that he and all the citizens of the Third Reich were among the passengers and that he had to make a choice between his religious faith and the demands of the political order that would make him another passenger on Nazism's train. To choose his faith required resistance.

'I would like to call out to everyone who is riding on this train,' he wrote in his journal, ' "Jump out of the train before it reaches its destination, even if it costs your life!" '

Like every able-bodied Austrian man, Franz Jägerstätter was called to do military service. His draft notice arrived in February 1943 when his oldest daughter was five. Ignoring the advice of his pastor and many others, he refused to take the military oath, and for this he was immediately jailed.

His act of resistance moved those in positions of political authority in surprising ways. He was offered the possibility of non-combatant service, but after carefully searching his conscience, Franz said that it was not possible for him to wear the uniform, no matter what his own responsibilities might be. This sealed his fate. He was finally condemned to death, and on August 6, 1943 — the Feast of the Transfiguration, and precisely two years before the atom bomb was dropped on Nagasaki — he was led from his cell in Berlin's Brandenburg Prison to the scaffold and was beheaded. He was 37.

His sacrifice was beyond measure: he loved life, his family, his fields, his neighbours. Perhaps hardest of all was the knowledge that he was making decisions abhorred by relatives and neighbours, and contrary to the advice of his pastor and bishop. (The bishop's views were unchanged even after the war. Recalling his meeting with Franz, he wrote: 'To no avail I set before [Jägerstätter] all the moral principles defining the responsibility carried by citizens and private individuals for the actions of civil authority . . . Jägerstätter represents a completely exceptional case, one more to be marvelled at than copied.')

How did Franz Jägerstätter — a devout Catholic who had been sexton of his parish church — dare to follow his conscience rather than accept the direction of his pastor and bishop? Franz's journal and letters from prison (published in 1964 as part of Gordon Zahn's book about Jägerstätter, *In Solitary Witness*), make clear his conviction that not only the community of believers, the church, but the *individual* believer is called to give witness, to prophesy and protest. Faith leads the believer to evaluate each choice in the light of eternity.

'Just as the man who thinks only of this world,' he wrote to his wife from prison, 'does everything possible to make life here easier and better, so must we too, who believe in the Eternal Kingdom, risk everything in order to receive a great reward there. Just as those who believe in National Socialism tell themselves that their struggle is for survival, so must we, too, convince ourselves that the struggle is for the Eternal Kingdom. But with this difference: we need no rifles or pistols for our battle but, instead, spiritual weapons. . . . The surest mark of the follower of Jesus is found in deeds showing love of neighbour. To do to one's neighbour what one would desire for oneself is more than merely not doing to others what one would not want done to oneself. Let us love our enemies, bless those who curse us, pray for those who persecute us. For love will conquer and endure for eternity. And happy are they who live and die in God's love.'

The prison chaplain in Berlin who was often with Franz until his execution said later: 'I can say with certainty that this simple man is the only saint I have ever met in my lifetime.'

When Franz Jägerstätter's story became known through Gordon Zahn's book during the Vietnam war, it helped encourage many draft-age American Christians to refuse military service. Through Archbishop Thomas Roberts, the retired Bishop of Bombay then living in London, the story made its way to the Second Vatican Council and helped the bishops endorse non-violence and conscientious objection. Now films have been made about Franz in both the United States and Germany. In December, 1984, the President of Austria, responding to a national petition, issued a posthumous Award of Honour to Franz Jägerstätter. On the 50th anniversary of their honeymoon trip to Rome, Franz's widow returned to Rome where she and the current Bishop of Linz (Jägerstätter's diocese) were given an audience with Pope John Paul II. The current Bishop of Linz, with the support of Cardinal Koenig of Vienna, is considering taking steps towards the official canonization of Franz Jägerstätter.

Times have changed. Yesterday's lonely dissenters, acting according to conscience and refusing the advice of church leaders, become today's saints.

The refusal to kill others can be, in some circumstances even more than others, a powerful witness. Yet conscientious objection is only the negative aspect of a positive commitment to care for the lives of others. Christian life is far more than the avoidance of evil. In the parable of the tidy but empty house, Jesus says:

> When the unclean spirit has gone out of a man, he passes through waterless places seeking rest, but he finds none. Then he says, 'I will return to the house from which I came.' And when he comes, he finds it empty, swept, and put in order. Then he goes and brings with him seven other spirits more evil than himself, and they enter and dwell there; and the last state of that man becomes worse than the first. (Matt. 12:43–45)

One can drive an evil spirit from one's life but, if nothing new and positive fills the space, a vacuum is created which not only draws back the exiled evil spirit but seven others even worse than the first. A vacuum cannot be filled with a vacuum; evil cannot be overcome with evil.

Responding to evil with its own weapons, though it can seem such an obvious good, results in a life that is centred on evil. Very often people who live in fear of armed men *become* armed men. They take up the same weapons and even adopt the characteristics and hated practises of the adversary. When the Nazi forces bombed cities, there was immense revulsion in Britain and the United States, but in the end the greatest acts of city destruction were done by Britain and the United States.

But what is one to do? Christians cannot be passive about those events and structures which cause suffering and death.

For centuries men and women have been searching for effective ways of both protecting life *and* combating evil. It is only in our own century, because of movements associated with such people as Gandhi, Martin Luther King, Dorothy Day and Lech Walesa, that non-violent struggle has become a recognized alternative to passivity on the one hand, and violence on the other.

One Christian whose life gives witness to the way of active non-violence is a cheerful Brazilian lawyer, Mario

Carvalho de Jesus. He is a married man and has seven children. Mario's religious conversion while still a student in Law School led him to commit his vocation to the poor. He went on to help found both *Servicio Paz y Justicia* (Service for Peace and Justice) and is among the founders of the *Frente Nacional do Trabalho* (the National Labour Front), a workers' organization for the application of Christian social teaching through active non-violence. His involvement with the poor and with unions made him a target of the former military regime, and he was often imprisoned.

Mario has a gift for reaching out in a friendly, disarming way to everyone, not least to his enemies. During a strike in 1958 when police were sent to attack the workers, Mario led the strikers chanting, 'Long live the police!' He went up to speak to them, saying, 'We are your brothers! Just as you have your uniform, we have our work clothes. If the law in Brazil were to protect rights, it would be *we* who would call you and ask you to come for our boss. But you needn't worry about us now that you're here. We will cause you no trouble. We will respect property and persons.' Then he went on to tell the police why the workers were striking. The police decided not to break up the demonstration. Happily, 46 days later the workers won the agreement they were seeking.

He has been no less friendly to prisonguards, or even been resentful about being in prison. 'Prison,' he says, 'gives me the opportunity to pass the message of the gospel on to the police!'

'We must not be afraid to be imprisoned or to give our lives,' he explains, 'because it is fear that strengthens the political system. Remember the apostles when they were in prison and beaten. The apostles were beaten, but they were glad to give testimony to the truth of Christ. We have to prepare non-violent activists to be pleased when they are imprisoned.'[28]

Mario has often explained active non-violence to others:

At first sight, the way of violence is the most impressive because it satisfies our aggresive impulses. But when you look at violence, you see that its promises never come true. At best, if you are lucky enough to be on the winning side, you find many of the peoples and places you wanted to protect are destroyed. You have a little space — this is called peace — before the next explosion. Violence also has the problem that it requires secrecy to be effective. You have clandestine meetings, and you have to distrust even the people you work with because there is always the chance that someone is a spy. Also, violence usually prevents the family from working together for social change. It is self-sacrificing, which can be a good thing, but it has a tendency to corrupt and of its nature it destroys. Violence is always in a hurry. It thrives on fear, rage, hatred and aggression. It uses lies. Also we find no example of killing in the life of Jesus. Rather you see him speaking out against violence.

But active non-violence does not seek the victory of one group over another but a change in which the whole society benefits. It is based on truth and love, not on domination. It is patient. It is willing to take time. It believes that, just as you and I have been converted so others, too, can be changed. Which of us is changed by threats? Rather than cause your enemy or innocent bystanders to suffer, the non-violent person takes the suffering and does everything possible to protect the innocent. With active non-violence, the whole family can take part, even the weak and old. We respect each person and believe each person has something good to do, something we all need. Non-violence is not killing, but healing. As doctors try to heal broken bodies, we try to heal broken communities. And with non-violence, we can always draw inspiration from the life of Jesus, who lives only by the truth and always gives us the example of healing.[29]

The power of non-violence to change both hearts and social structures has been repeatedly demonstrated since ancient times. But especially in recent years, as the technology of violence has made war more dangerous than any evil it could be directed against, non-violent approaches to conflict resolution have been taken up by those who struggle for human rights and social justice.

How different the recent struggle for democracy in the Philippines would have been had it not been for the non-violent commitment of so many people. In the final months before Ferdinand Marcos' withdrawal, 'tent cities' for prayer and non-violent training were set up in various centres of population. Returning from a visit with leaders of the non-violent training movement in the Philippines, Hildegard Goss-Mayr wrote:

> One tent was set in a little park right in the banking centre in Manila, where the financial power of the Marcos regime was concentrated. Around the prayer tent, people who promised to fast and pray would, day and night, have a presence and carry within their fast and their prayer the whole revolutionary process. And I think we cannot emphasize this enough: that in this whole process, there was always this unity of outward non-violent action against the unjust regime and of that deep spirituality that gave people the strength later on to stand up against the tanks and to confront the tanks: this force of fasting and prayer. And in the celebrations of the Eucharist, they would point out that we are not fighting against flesh and blood, we are fighting against the demons of richness and exploitation and hatred that we have to cast out . . . from ourselves, from the military, from Marcos and his followers . . . It makes a great difference . . . whether you promote hatred and revenge, or whether you help the people to stand firmly for justice but at the same time not to let themselves be taken in by hatred for those who stand with the oppressor . . . [you learn] to stand for justice *and* to love your enemy . . . to the

extent that you want to be liberated, you *want* to liberate him, you want to win him, you want to draw him in. You don't want his destruction but his liberation.[30]

It was precisely that spirit that led hundreds of thousands of unarmed people to fill the streets, block the tanks, and to reach out as brothers and sisters to the soldiers. 'You are one of us,' they said again and again. 'You belong to the people.' In the case of one detachment of soldiers sent to take control of a television station, shooting their way in if necessary, the people blocking the entrance greeted the soldiers and presented them with hamburgers and cokes bought at a nearby McDonalds stand. The soldiers ate the hamburgers and went back to their barracks.

9: A life of recognizing Jesus

Dorothy Day often repeated a saying of St. John of the Cross: 'Love is the measure by which we shall be judged.' This summarizes much of the gospel, and has to do with God's final weighing of our lives:

When the Son of man comes in his glory, and all the angels with him, then he will sit on his glorious throne. Before him will be gathered all the nations, and he will separate them one from another as a shepherd separates the sheep from the goats, and he will place the sheep at his right hand, but the goats at the left. Then the King will say to those on his right hand, 'Come, O blessed of my Father, inherit the kingdom prepared for you from the foundation of the world; for I was hungry and you gave me food, I was thirsty and you gave me drink, I was a stranger and you welcomed me, I was naked and you clothed me, I was sick and you visited me, I was in prison and you came to me.' Then the righteous will answer him, 'Lord, when did we see you hungry and feed you . . . ?' And the King will answer them, 'Truly I say to you, as you did it to one of the least of these my brethren, you did it to me.' Then he will say to those at his left hand, 'Depart from me, you cursed, into the eternal fire prepared for the devil and his angels; for I was hungry and you gave me no food . . .' Then they will answer, 'Lord, when did we see you hungry . . . and did not minister to you?' Then he will answer them, 'Truly, I say to you, as you did it not to one of the least of these, you did it not to me.' (Matt. 25:31–46)

In practically any ancient church in Europe, one finds at least one visual representation of the Last Judgement, the blessed processing off complacently to the left, the damned — rather pathetic figures — being shovelled by grotesque devils into the fiery jaws of a dragon.

On the south porch of the Cathedral of Our Lady at Chartres, in France, one of the world's most unhellish places, this scene is carved in stone. In medieval times, the stone was brilliantly painted. The effect must have been stunning — and perhaps alarming. In Moscow's Kremlin, over the entrance to the Cathedral of St. Michael the Archangel, summoner of the Last Judgement, there is a large icon portraying the same scene.

At both churches, I have heard similar answers to the question: 'Why are we judged together and not one by one when we die?'

It is because each person's life is far from finished with death. Our acts of love and failures to love continue to have consequences until the end of history. What Adam and Eve did, what Moses did, what Herod did, what Pilate did, what the Apostles did, what Caesar did, what Hitler did, what Martin Luther King did, what Dorothy Day did — all these lives continue to matter and have particular consequences every single day. This same principle applies equally to the least person. What you and I do, and what we fail to do, will matter forever.

It weighs heavily on many people that Jesus preached not only of heaven but also of hell. There are quite a lot of references to hell in the gospels, many of them in the Sermon on the Mount. How can a loving God allow a place devoid of love?

The only response to that question which makes sense to me was a sermon I heard in an old gothic church in Prague in 1964, during an assembly of the Christian Peace Conference. The preacher was a particularly courageous man who has seen a great deal of prison from the inside. It is now too many years for me to repeat accurately what he said, but this is what I remember of it, or perhaps what it has become to mean for me in the passage of nearly 25 years.

God allows us to go wherever we are going. We are not forced to love. We are not forced to recognize God's presence. It is all an invitation. We can choose. Perhaps, in God's mercy, we can even make the choice of heaven in hell. But very likely we will make the same kinds of choices after death that we made before death. In *The Great Divorce*, C.S. Lewis has a tour bus leaving daily from hell to heaven; it is never full and it tends to return with as many passengers as it took on the trip out of hell.

Anyone reading this with more than one white hair knows that, the older we are, the more we live by old choices, and defend those choices, and make ideologies, philosophies, even theologies out of our choices. We canonize our choices by repetition.

We can say not just once, but forever, 'I do not know the man'. We can say he is worthless, has no one to blame for his troubles but himself, that his problems are not our business, that he is an enemy, that he deserves to die.

If I cannot find the face of Jesus in the face of those who are my enemies, if I cannot find him in the unbeautiful, if I cannot find him in those who have the 'wrong ideas', if I cannot find him in the poor and the defeated, how will I find him in bread and wine, or in the life after death? If I do not reach out in this world to those with whom he has identified himself, why do I imagine that I will want to be with him, and them, in heaven? Why would I want to be for all eternity in the company of those I avoided every day of my life?

The Peaceable Kingdom would be hell for those who avoided peace and devoted their lives to division.

Teaching about the Last Judgement, Jesus describes the coming together of every last person who has ever lived, the vast majority of them needing to be raised from the dead for the event. This taxes the imagination. It is nearly as hard to believe as creation itself and the surprise of life.

At the heart of what Jesus says in every act and parable

is this: Now, this minute, we can be on the way to the
Peaceable Kingdom. The way into it is simply to live in
awareness of God's presence in those around us. Doing
that, we learn the truth of what St. Catherine of Siena said:
'All the way to heaven *is* heaven, because Jesus said, "I am
the way." ' (One could add, 'and all the way to hell *is* hell'.
To the extent I fail to love, hell is in my life already.)

Perhaps there have been church people who occasionally
have admitted to disappointment over Jesus' teaching on
the Last Judgement. Could he not have said something
about the advantages of having been baptized and
belonging to the right church? Wouldn't this have been the
right place for Jesus to have said, 'If you want to inherit
eternal life, confess me as Lord and Saviour and be saved'?
Couldn't he have said that the Last Judgement would be a
theological test and those who got the right answers would
get the ultimate high grades?

It seems Jesus is not a leading institutionalist. The churches are probably among his heaviest burdens.

Then what is the whole point of the church? Doesn't the
church matter?

Two black women, Celie and Shug, discuss this question
in Alice Walker's novel, *The Colour Purple:*

'You telling me God love you.' Celie says to Shug, 'and
you ain't never done nothing for him? I mean not go to
church, not sing in the choir, feed the preacher and all like
that?'

'But if God love me, Celie,' Shug responds, 'I don't have
to do all that. Unless I want to. There's a lot of things I
can do that I speck God likes.'

'Like what?'

'Oh, I can lay back and admire stuff. Be happy. Have a
good time.'

'Well, this sounds like blasphemy sure nuff.'

'Celie,' Shug says, 'tell the truth, have you ever found
God in church? I never did. I just found a bunch of folks
hoping for him to show. Any God I ever felt in church I

brought in with me. And I think the other folks did too. They come to *share* God, not find God.'[31]

Church membership will not save us, yet we need the church. We need the church, the community of belivers, as a place of sharing God. We need a place to gather where it isn't considered strange to talk about God or to care about the gospels. We need the church as a school of holiness — holiness meaning: living in the mercy of God. We need the church because we need to be part of a community of praise, remembrance, reflection, a community seeking to be aware of God's presence in the world and in our lives. We need the church because Jesus has said he is with us whenever two or three gather together in his name. We need the church because he called us to recognize him in bread broken and wine poured out. We need the church because we need a community that will help us learn to respond to people we might otherwise despise and treat as enemies. We need the church to help us see beyond, and reach beyond, national borders. We need a community of faith to help us experience God's mercy and forgiveness when, like those who proceeded the Samaritan on the road to Jericho, we find ourselves living blind, merciless lives, unaware that Jesus is hidden in those we avoid or are ready to destroy. We need to be within the community of believers as a place of remembrance of Jesus' life and words. We need the church because we need each other.

Yet we have to be on guard about the church's tendency to make an idol of itself, to be pleased with itself, and to consign to hell those who don't fit. We need to be on guard about the church's tendency — our own tendency — to forget or explain away or bury in footnotes the more inconvenient parts of the gospel.

Whatever church we are part of, we need to remember what Jesus himself says matters most.

He asks us to recognize him in the least person.

He says there will be those who do so even though they aren't aware of him and think they have denied him. Yet their merciful care for others is enough. They are welcomed into the kingdom 'prepared for you from the foundation of the world.'

His kingdom opens itself to us not because we deserve it or belong to the right church (or any church), or have remarkable intelligence, or are theologically astute, or write religious books, or achieve recognition, or because we know bishops, or even know saints.

The kingdom receives us, Jesus says, because we are willing to care for the hungry, the thirsty, the homeless, the naked, the sick and the imprisoned. We are saved because we care for unattractive strangers, annoying relatives, even those who threaten us. We are saved because we allow the mercy of God not just to enter our lives, as if one's life were private property and God a personal acquisition, but because we let God's mercy pass through our lives.

We are saved because we respond to others as if they were Jesus.

10: An old woman and a man with a gun

Can anyone really live out this kind of love? There are so many examples of all sorts of people opening their lives and hearts to others that the answer is certainly Yes. While history books tend to emphasize wars and warriors, and newspapers are far more likely to feature murder than life saving, remarkably few people are pathologically violent. Millions of people, in refusing to go the way of destruction, manage to live lives that centre on the care of others, responding as if their guests were Jesus himself. There are many signs in the world of the activity of the Holy Spirit, so many in fact that one dares to think that the main reformation in Christian history is not in the past but in the present. Churches have increasingly grown beyond national identification. In the past there were several smaller churches that were called Peace Churches, but today there are signs that the Church as a whole and not only scattered fragments of it is becoming the Peace Church it was always intended to become. We live in a time when there are large movements of people, many of them motivated by their religious faith, who have come together to build bridges between enemies and to develop non-violent methods of conflict resolution.

It is amazing what a difference a few people make. In fact it is astonishing what can come out of the faith of just one person.

One of my favourite parables of what ordinary human beings can be is about a woman I know of only through a news story I happened to read in *The Christian Century*. Mrs. Louise Degrafinried, 73 years old at the time, lives with her husband, Nathan, in Mason, Tennessee. They belong to the Mount Sinai Primitive Baptist Church.

One morning Riley Arzeneaux, a man who had just escaped from prison with four other inmates, came into their house. He aimed a shot gun at Louise and Nathan and shouted, 'Don't make me kill you!'

Louise responded to this nightmarish event as calmly as mothers normally respond to all the crises and accidents that happen in a house full of children.

'Young man,' she said, 'I am a Christian lady. I don't believe in violence. Put down that gun and you sit down. I don't allow no violence here.' He put the weapon on the couch. While she had Nathan get the unexpected guest some dry socks, she made breakfast: bacon and eggs, toast, milk and coffee. She put put her best napkins.

When the three of them sat down to eat, she took Riley's hand in her own and said, 'Young man, let's give thanks that you came here and that you are safe.' She said a prayer and asked him if there was anything he would like to say to the Lord. He couldn't think of anything so she said to him, 'Just say, "Jesus wept." ' (She was later asked how she happened to choose that text. 'Because I figured that he didn't have no church background, so I wanted to start him off simple; something short, you know.')

After breakfast she held his hand again. He was trembling all over. 'Young man, I love you and God loves you. God loves all of us, every one of us, especially you. Jesus died for you because he loves you so much.'

Then the police arrived. Hearing the approaching sirens, the man said, 'They gonna kill me when they get here'. But Louise said she was going out to talk to them. Standing on her porch, she spoke to the police in the same terms she had spoken to the convict: 'Y'all put those guns away. I don't allow no violence here.'

The police were as docile in their response to this authoritative grandmother as the convict had been. They put their guns back in their holsters. Soon afterward, the convict was taken back to the prison. No one was harmed.

The story of what happened to two of the other escaped convicts is a familiar tragedy. They came upon a family preparing a barbecue in their backyard. The husband, having heard about the escaped prisoners on the radio, had armed himself with a pistol. He tried to use it but was himself shot dead. The men took his wife hostage, stole the family car, and managed to drive out of the state before they were captured and the woman freed.[32]

Louise and Nathan Degrafinried might also have been killed, of course. Good, decent people die tragically every day. But actually it isn't so surprising that their gentle welcome to a frightened man provided them with more security than any gun.

It may be that both the prisoner and the police who encountered Louise that day thank God for meeting her and now have an altogether different idea of what it can mean to be human than they had before. Perhaps they live quite different lives because one old Christian woman does in fact love her enemies.

Notes

1. *A Testament of Hope: The Essential Writings of Martin Luther King*, edited by James Washington; Harper & Row
2. *The Asia Journal of Thomas Merton*, paper on 'Monastic Experience and East-West Dialogue,' pp 309–317
3. *Conjectures of A Guilty Bystander*, Thomas Merton; Doubleday, New York; pp 156–158
4. Introduction to the Japanese edition of Thomas Merton's autobiography, *The Seven Storey Mountain:* included in *Introductions East & West; The Foreign Prefaces of Thomas Merton*, Unicorn Press, Greensboro, North Carolina
5. *The Hidden Ground of Love: Letters of Thomas Merton*, edited by William Shannon; Farrar Straus Giroux, New York; pp 294–7; also see *Thomas Merton's Struggle With Peacemaking*, James Forest; Benet Press, 6101 East Lake Rd., Erie, Pa. 16511; *Thomas Merton: Prophet in the Belly of a Paradox*, ed. Gerald Twomey, Paulist Press
6. *A Precocious Autobiography*, Yevgeny Yevtushenko, Collins, London
7. *Christianity and Class War*, Nicholas Berdyaev; Sheed & Ward, London
8. *The Catholic Worker*, October 1961; 36 East First St., New York, N.Y. 10003; also note references for endnote 5, above
9. The story of 'how goodness happened' in Le Chambon is told by Philip Hallie in *Lest Innocent Blood Be Shed*, Harper & Row, New York

10. *Clement of Alexandria: Selections from The Protreptikos*, Thomas Merton, New Directions Books, New York
11. *St. John Chrysostom*, Donald Attwater, Harvill Press, London
12. Author interview with Fr. Chacour; in somewhat similar form it appears in *Blood Brothers*, Elias Chacour, Zondervan, Grand Rapids, Michigan; also see *IFOR Report*, December 1980; International Fellowship of Reconciliation, Spoorstraat 38, 1815 BK Alkmaar, The Netherlands
13. *Love is the Measure: A Biography of Dorothy Day*, Jim Forest; Paulist Press, Ramsey, New Jersey; Marshall Pickering, Basingstoke pp 91–92
14. *The Monk of Mount Athos: Staretz Silouan* by Archimandrite Sophrony; Mowbrays, London
15. ibid.
16. *Earth's Answer*, Russell Schweickhart; Harper & Row, New York
17. *The Face of Prayer*, Abraham Menashe; Knopf, New York
18. *My Childhood*, Maxim Gorky, Penguin Books, London
19. Interview by the author and Diane Leonetti with Alfred Hassler, published in abridged form in *Fellowship* magazine, September 1974; Fellowship of Reconciliation, Box 271, Nyack, N.Y. 10960
20. *The Hidden Ground of Love: Letters by Thomas Merton*, edited by William Shannon; Farrar Straus Giroux, New York; p 264
21. *Reconciliation International*, February 1987; International Fellowship of Reconciliation, Spoorstraat 38, 1815 BK Alkmaar, The Netherlands
22. *The Jewish War*, II, 16, 4; Penguin Books, London
23. *Martin Luther King: A Documentary*, edited by Flip Schulke; Norton & Co., New York
24. *The Wisdom of the Desert*, Thomas Merton; New Directions, New York
25. *Reconciliation International*, April 1986

26. *Conjectures of a Guilty Bystander*, Thomas Merton, Doubleday & Co., New York; p 12
27. *The Hidden Ground of Love: Letters of Thomas Merton*, edited by William Shannon; Farrar Straus Giroux, New York; p 272
28. Interview by Marty Deming, *IFOR Report*, September 1981
29. From an unpublished interview with author, Alkmaar, summer 1981
30. *Reconciliation International*, April 1986; also see *Commonweal*, 'Non-violence in the Philippines: The Precarious Road', June 20, 1986; 15 Dutch St., New York, N.Y. 10038
31. *The Colour Purple*, Alice Walker; Harcourt Brace Jovanovich, New York, p 176. Women's Press, London
32. 'Bless You, Mrs. Degrafinried,' William H. Willimon, *Christian Century*, March 14, 1984

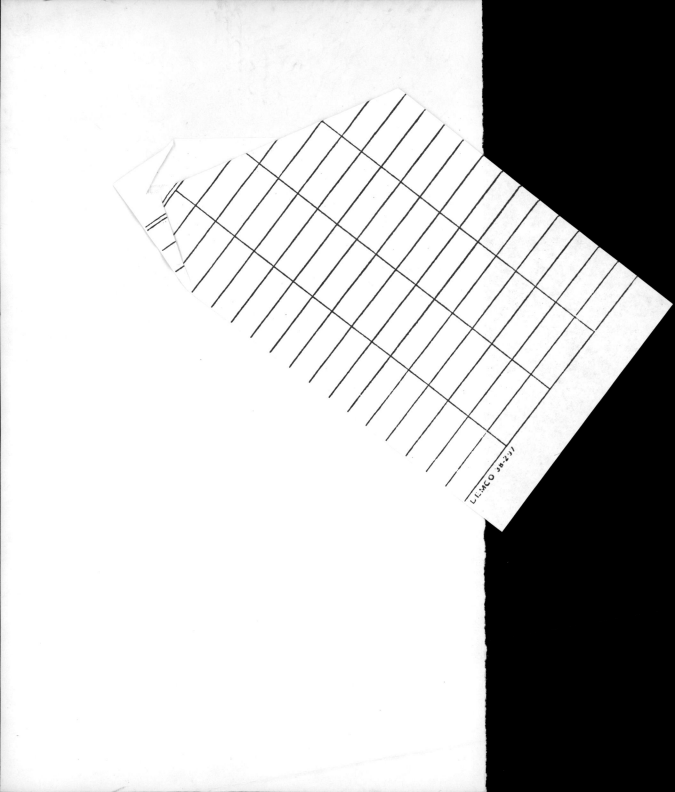